So Mammy Said

By
Patrick Burke

PUBLISH AMERICA

PublishAmerica
Baltimore

First printing

ISBN: 1-4137-7478-4
PUBLISHED BY PUBLISHAMERICA, LLLP
www.publishamerica.com
Baltimore

Printed in the United States of America

Dedication

This book is dedicated to my grandchildren, Liam and Noreen, who only came to us for a short while but are forever in our hearts.

Acknowledgments

I owe a debt of gratitude to six wonderful people.

My lovely wife Patricia, (aka) Kitty, who stood with me through thick and thin including every misspelled word and grammatical error.

My daughter Marie who has helped me tremendously with this book and who is a cup of sunshine to us all.

My loving children Siobhán, Seán, and Kevin who love me for who I am.

My sister Dr. Margaret McGrath who excels in her field of endeavor.

I am also grateful to countless other people. They should know who they are and if they don't, then I'm not grateful to them at all.

Sure yis are all just great and I love yis te death!

Chapter One

The Question

"Which would you rather do: run a mile, suck a boil, or eat a bag of scabs?" George Scally asks me.

"What do you think, stupid? Run a mile, of course."

"And supposing you had no legs, which would you rather do?"

Well, that does it. He can't stick to the question like anyone else. Just like the question: "curse a witch, jump a ditch, or swim a mile up stream." No, Scally has to put his own wording to it, like this having no legs business. Always adding something stupid that isn't a part of the thing to begin with. So I tell him what I would do.

"I'd close my fist and lay it on the butt of your jaw so it would shut your big feckin mouth once and for all."

He jumps up from the desk we both share in the classroom. I make the same move and we go into our fighting poses.

"I dare ya to close my big mouth! Come on, I dare ya, I double dare ya," he says.

Our teacher, Mrs. O'Kelly, calls the two of us up front where she's smothering the fire with her fat legs. She gives us each two slaps for talking in class, and then asks us what we were talking about.

I say, "Nothing, ma'am."

She repeats, "Nothing ma'am" in a singsong voice and says, "Now we all know it's impossible to talk about nothing. I saw the two of you talking, and everyone in this classroom knows, except for a few morons, that all conversation must have a subject matter."

I don't know what a subject matter is, but I do know if she heard us talking, then she must know what we were talking about, so why does she have to ask.

"Paidin Burke, I will ask you again, what were you talking about?" She removes her steel-rimmed glasses and holds them up toward the light from the window. I can see white lines from her eyes to both ears where the steel frames sank into the flesh of her fat face. It's as though her face tried to grow over her glasses like barbed wire around a tree.

"He asked me a question, ma'am."

Nodding, she says, "Very good, now we're getting somewhere." She brings the glasses towards her mouth, blows on them, and proceeds to wipe them with her handkerchief. "What question did he ask you?"

With my head down, I mumble, "He asked me if I would rather run a mile, suck a boil, or eat a bag of scabs, ma'am."

Looking like she could chew nails, she demands, "And what was your answer?"

"Run a mile, ma'am."

She turns her attention to George. "Is that right?"

"Yes, ma'am, but he also cursed."

I think to myself, if he tells on me again to save himself, I will kill him as dead as a doornail for sure. He does that all the time, and he's getting more like a girl every day. Girls always tell tales to the teacher. The last time the class was outside on the grass, the two of us were trying to put straws up Marie Mulvaney's legs. She drew back and hit him, but I was the one who got slapped because he kept a straight face and I couldn't. And the time he pushed a straw up a frog and blew him up till he was like a balloon, did I tell on him? No way, I'm not a squealer like him. Now here he is again, up to his auld dirty tricks. Well, this will be the last time he'll ever do it, because I'll beat the living be Jasus out of him. I'll leave his eyebrows walking around like hairy maggots, and then I'll sit with Liam Mahon. Liam and I are kinda friends, but he lives down in Puttingham and that's too far away to play in the evenings. Yes, I owe George Scally a good few clouts.

Now she's glaring at me. "What curse word did he use?"

"He used the 'F' word, ma'am."

She turns to me. "What 'F' word did you use?"

I stutter for a second, and then I blabber out the only word that comes to me. "Fun, ma'am."

"Fun?" she says, and I can tell she doesn't believe me. She confirms this quickly. "Well, I don't believe you. Now I'm not sure what word you used, but if it's the one I'm thinking of, it's a vile word that borders on a one-way ticket to damnation. There are poor souls suffering in hell today because of words like that, and I will not tolerate them in my school." She gives me two more slaps with her stick, and tells me when the priest comes, she will single me out for his special attention. She tells George he would get more only he didn't lie or swear. She sends us back to our seats, and I can't wait till we get out for lunch to give George the best beating he ever got.

And come to think of it, it was him that picked out that new fancy stick for Mrs. O'Kelly last week. Every now and then she orders one of us to get a new stick when hers goes missing. Only George couldn't get a small one like everyone else does. No, it had to be the bare best, an ash sucker half as thick as my wrist and nearly three feet long. It hurts like Billy-be-damned, especially if she gets you across the thumb with it. He must have spent all weekend working on it. It's nice and round where he peeled the skin off and pared the little knots to make it smooth. He was so proud of that stick when he brought it in to her Monday, but as fate would have it wasn't he the first one to get slapped with it for not knowing his sums? It was good enough for him, and I was delighted.

She doesn't send me to get a stick anymore, because the last one I got took over an hour. She wanted to know if I had to go to Ballymahon (six miles away) for it. I used the time to go home, which only took me five minutes. There, I ate the last of the bread before going back to school, and then I picked up a piece of a bramble that had blown down off a tree and gave it to her. It was so small and thin you couldn't kill a fly with it, unless you hit him right. She said she was surprised I was able to carry it. I don't think she meant that.

Finally, we get out for lunch and I run home, but there's only stir-a-bout made from Indian meal, also known as Peeler's brimstone. It's bright yellow and the grains are small and hard, and the taste would turn an ass from his oats. Smiler Cormack, the closest thing to a philosopher that our village has to offer, says it's no wonder the Indians are yellow. I wouldn't know because I've never seen an Indian in our village. Mammy says the English first brought it into the country during the famine to feed people when they were dying of hunger. Nowadays it's mostly used to feed cattle and pigs, but here in the village we use Peeler's brimstone in our houses because the flour is sent to England where everything is still rationed following the war.

It's not too bad as stir-a-bout when we have fresh buttermilk to go with it. Sometimes Mammy bakes a cake with it, but the cakes taste like shite, especially with margarine. Our margarine is nearly as yellow as the Indian meal, and tastes worse. The margarine is tolerable when used to fry bread; but even then we use lots of salt and pepper to kill the taste. Watt, my older brother, says it's only fit to grease axles.

I gobble down all I can anyway, and head back to school. By the time I get there, children are forming a ring for the fight. Most are rooting for me, because they know Scally squealed on me. We both get in the ring and circle each other in our fighting poses. We've done this many times before, but this time will be different. No more threats and no more of the "I dare ya, I double dare ya." I know just what I'm going to do—and I do it. I step in and land one right on his nose. He starts to bleed, and then the eejit stops to look at the blood on his hand. I lay another on him. He's bent over with his head in his hands, and I give him a good kick on the shin. Now he's roaring like a stuck pig and I lay into him with both fists. The ring of children pull me off him and declare, "Pat Burke is the winner." It only lasted a few minutes because I took him by surprise.

I feel good and enjoy all the backslapping, and I think to myself, now who's the cock, and who's the turkey, and who's king of the roost? We make up later when Mrs. O'Kelly asks what happened to his face and he tells her he fell playing leap frog.

The priest came a week later and had his usual bread, jam, biscuits, and tea from Mrs. O'Kelly's best china. She must have forgotten to tell him about me, because he never said a thing. I was about twelve years old at the time.

Moyvore School 1951, Patrick Burke is sixth from the right in the middle row.

The Beginning

I was born in rural Ireland on April 1, 1938. A fool's day indeed. By the time I arrived on the scene, my mother had been on the delivery bed eleven times, bringing forth six sisters and five brothers. Their names are Maureen, Dolly, Cathy, Tom, Joe, Watt, Seán,

Margaret, Teresa, Chris, Anne, and myself Pat. Two more would come after that—Frank and Eddie. Teresa's twin sister Bernadette died at age two.

My father Joseph Burke was, as my mother always said, an independent man beholden to no one other than God. He would never work for anyone other than himself, so it seemed appropriate that he should become a blacksmith.

He didn't start out planning to be a blacksmith. He was training to become a veterinarian when both his parents passed away. Both he and his brother and sister then went to live with an aunt who couldn't afford to send him to school. That's when he decided to become a blacksmith.

Before they died, my father's parents had been evicted from their farm near Kilbeggan for nonpayment of taxes. My grandfather, Walter Burke, then went to work as a cooper for Locks Distillery in Killbeggan, and progressed to the position of foreman. My grandmother's maiden name was O'Brien and she was an elementary school teacher.

In those days, an apprentice was required to pay for his training, and as my father didn't have any money, he worked for his employer two extra years without wages. Having completed the seven years required of him, he applied for the position of village blacksmith in Moyvore and got the job. That's where he met my mother, Bridget McCann, who worked as a shop girl in Grennans' pub and grocery. My father was thirty-four years old and she was twenty-one.

And so the stage was set, the seeds were sown, and a journey begun. My father was an independent man of means who would never work for anyone other than himself—and so my Mammy said.

Flight in the Night

One of my earliest memories is walking behind the ass and cart our family borrowed to move to our new home—a council house provided by the local government to those who were less well off. Some people objected to my father getting it. They claimed that a self-employed tradesman like my father wasn't entitled to it, and the house should be given to a laboring man. Those objections were overcome with the help of the health board and some input from Doctor Joyce, the local doctor. I never knew whether it was the unhealthy conditions in our other house or the sheer size of my family that prompted him to intervene.

Before we moved, the owner of the terraced house where we were living offered to sell it to my father for eighty pounds. He refused on the grounds that the floor was rotten and the roof would need to be replaced within a few years. Years later I was told that my father didn't have the money to put a down payment on it, never mind buy it.

It's late at night and my brothers and sisters are going in and out of the house loading beds and clothing on the cart. Daddy has borrowed the ass and cart from Smiler Cormack to make the move to our new house. The little village of Moyvore is quiet; the only sounds come from the Burkes.

Located in the center of Ireland, our village lies on the main road between Mullingar and Ballymahon. It consists of two pubs and grocery shops, one butcher shop, a post office, a forge, and seven houses. All these buildings are on one side of the street, with a single farm house on the opposite side.

Mammy keeps making a shushing noise and tells us to be quiet. She doesn't want us to wake up the neighbors. All the village houses are dark and even the two pubs have closed up for the night. I keep rubbing my eyes to get the sleep out of them.

Mammy sends my sister Margaret upstairs to make sure we got everything. Margaret comes running back down the stairs and her face is all white. She runs to Mammy and puts her arms around her. "I saw him! I saw him, Mammy!" she blurts out.

"What's the matter with you, child, you saw what?"

"The white horse on the wall, Mammy. He was there on the end wall."

Mammy tells her, "Don't be so silly. It's probably just a shadow from the moon coming in the skylight."

Mammy takes her by the hand and goes toward the stairs. "Now you come up with me and I'll show you there's no horse or anything else in that room."

The two of them go upstairs and come down almost right away. Daddy looks at Mammy with a grin and asks her, "Are ya all right? Yis both look like ye'd seen a ghost."

Mammy says, "I'm all right, Joe." She gives one last look at the almost dead fire in the grate to make sure it's safe to leave. Finally we're all loaded up and ready to move to our new house. Mammy says, "Let's get out of here."

Years later, I was told that my older brothers and sisters liked to scare us younger children with stories of the white horse. No doubt, Mammy and Daddy were in on it and were having a good laugh when we weren't looking.

My father and mother are up at the front, walking and holding hands. He has the reins of the ass in his right hand, leading us on. We're all trudging behind three and four abreast. We're reduced in numbers because Maureen and Kitty (Cathy) have gone to work in England. I walk in the front row with Anne to my right, and to her right is Dolly carrying our baby brother Frank. I'm just a few feet from the back of the cart, where the frames of our mattresses stick out the back. There's also a black trunk with its round lid that acts as a bed and cradle for Frank. The wooden table balances on top, tied with a rope, and blankets and old clothes are stuffed in between. The load seems so high, I wonder if it is touching the sky.

Everyone who's old enough is carrying something, including the chairs and the long stool. Thousands of stars wink down at us, and my sister Teresa whispers to me, "They're little candles put there by God to show us the way." Frost on the road appears to give off little sparkles in the bright moonlight. I smell wafts of smoke from Daddy's pipe as it drifts back toward us.

Not a word is spoken as we walk along on our journey. Off in the distance I hear the craking of a corncrake. The only other sound is the rattle of cartwheels. As we pass Smiler Cormack's little thatched house, the ass keeps pulling toward it wanting to go home. Daddy gives a few sharp jerks on the winkers and the ass straightens out again.

A few hundred yards east of the village lies the green—a long, narrow strip of public land about an acre and a half in size. The local football team uses this land for practice and every once in awhile a traveling carnival or show performs there. Across from the green is the Kirk. It was once a protestant church. Now it is used for plays and concerts. As we pass the center of the green, I notice two tinkers' tents with the smoldering embers of a fire between them. A hobbled piebald pony munches hay beside their cart.

My feet are cold. I'm tired and falling behind. Anne takes my hand, but I pull back in defiance. She calls me a little spoiled brat. As we near the top of a big hill, someone says we're almost there. I battle bravely on till I can't walk anymore, and finally I give in and the tears start to flow.

Someone steps from behind, swoops me into his arms, and carries me the rest of the way. It's my brother Seán. The total journey is one third of a mile and I am two years old.

Years later, I could see similarities between our move and the flight of the holy family into Egypt. Both families moved at night so as not to be noticed. Each of the families were led by men named Joseph. One family fled the wrath of a depraved king, and the other that of an angry landlord. Both used an ass for the trip. And while the Palestinian ass had a heavy load to bear with Mary and Jesus, he wasn't burdened like the poor auld ass from Moyvore. Nor did he have a family of thirteen depending on him.

Chapter Two

Our New House

Our new house has three bedrooms and a kitchen in the center that takes up one third of the house. Our only cupboard is to the right of the fireplace—it's about two feet wide and has two shelves. The cupboard stands four feet off the floor and the door on it reaches the ceiling. Underneath is an open space where we stack turf and firewood.

The kitchen has two windows, one in front and one in back. Our kitchen furnishings consist of one large wooden table beside the back window. We also have four chairs and two long stools, plus the pine dresser and a long table. The top shelf of the dresser holds Mammy's two willow pattern dishes that Granny gave her as a wedding present. The other shelves hold dinner plates, saucers, and jam jars. The shelves contain hooks for hanging our cups and tin mugs.

Two doors lead off from the kitchen—one goes to my parents' bedroom, where they sleep along with baby Frank who sleeps in the lid of their black trunk. This room spans the full width of the house, has two windows, and is the same size as the kitchen.

The other door leads to a narrow hallway and two other rooms. The largest of these is at the back, and that's where I sleep with my five brothers. Tom, Joe, and Watt sleep in the newer and bigger bed while Seán, Chris, and I sleep in the older one.

We call this the practice bed, because at one time or another all of us have peed in it. The beds are just a few inches apart and there's barely room to walk around them.

The other room we call the box room. It's so small the double bed touches the walls on three sides. Margaret, Teresa, and Anne sleep in this one. Dolly has gone to work for Colonel Winter as a child's nurse and so she stays there.

For most of the first year, the talk in our house is mostly about the coldness of it. The wind blows right through the windows and under the door.

Our House

Builders

Daddy says the men who built this house were not tradesmen, but botchers. Most days, the chimney smokes so badly that we have to open the windows. This makes the house like a funnel, and there seems to be more smoke going out the windows than up the chimney. Most of my brothers have coughs, snots, and runny noses. Watt claims we'd be better off outside—that way we'd only have the cold to put up with. Tom says we have two choices: choke from the smoke or freeze to death. I don't want to do either one. I want to live to be as old and as big as Anne. That way she won't be always picking on me.

On frosty nights, the windows freeze over and we can't see out in the morning. The window frames are made from metal and when we try to open them they make a cracking noise from the ice. Tom forces one of them open and breaks the glass. Daddy calls him a stupid fool for not waiting till they thaw out from the heat of the fire.

"Sure I could wait," says Tom, "but by the look of that fire we could all be smothered by then."

Mammy complains about having to cook on a fire that's always smoking. She says when the windows are open, ashes get blown all over the frying pan. She says we should get a range or some sort of a cooker. Daddy tries to convince her the fire will stop smoking when the walls dry out.

She answers, "God only knows when that might happen. It's like saying, 'live horse and you'll get grass.'" Then he adds, "Sure the bloody eejits built the walls out of solid cement. Then again what more could one expect around here?"

Inside the fireplace is a grate with a hob on each side and a pit underneath to hold the ashes. Daddy took out the grate, because he said, "It burns too much turf and firewood when the air gets under it." He brought a flat piece of metal up from the forge and placed it over the pit. We build the fire on top, and it takes ages to light.

There's shiny green paint on the kitchen walls as far up as I can reach, and water is always running down it from the damp. Above the green paint, the walls are papered up to the ceiling. The wallpaper has damp patches all over, except near the fireplace. Margaret and Teresa write on the green paint and draw pictures with their fingers. Sometimes this winds up with them fighting because one or the other isn't happy with the drawing. Mammy gives them a scelp with the dishcloth to keep their minds on what she says are better things.

Margaret complains her hair stuck to the wall under the window in her room. She said she went to sleep with her head too close to the wall and her hair froze with the ice. Some of her hair is still on the wall. Everyone thinks this is funny, and Seán says, "The wall will be all red now, because her hair is red." Then he tells her, "What a pity your face wasn't against it as well, and we could have a freckled wall. We could even call it the red freckled room."

She says, " I may have red hair and freckles, but at least I'm not all a grizzle like you, you long hank of misery."

Seán has black curly hair like Tom, but he's not nearly as big and blocky. He's more the tall, gangly type. He was showing off his arm muscles when someone started saying he was all a grizzle. After that, he was teased about it regularly.

There are three redheads in our family: Joe, Watt, and Margaret. Teresa has blond hair and Anne's is brown. They're all completely different in looks. Teresa's short and weakly, while Anne is tall and gangly. Margaret is round and chubby, and the rest of us tease her with the rhyme, "Redhead, diddle de bob, kiss the divil upon the hob." It drives her mad which, of course, only makes us do it all the more. The rest of us have black hair, some curly, some straight.

Chris, like Teresa, is the second weakling of the family and suffers from asthma. He's always sucking his thumb, and at the same time he lays his forefinger across his nose while trying to curl his hair with his middle finger. He has a continuous wheeze from his asthma that Doctor Joyce says he'll get rid off when he becomes a teenager. Sometimes we call him "suck a diddy bull calf" because of his constant thumb-sucking.

Other than those differences, we seem to be much alike, and we do things in pairs. By this I mean work, fight, and play games. Seán and Chris are always playing kicking mules. They lie on their backs on the bed and flail at each other with their feet till one of them is on the floor. The loser has to go to Rooney's for the jug of milk.

The Rooneys live about two hundred yards from us, one of three houses at the crossroads. They're farmers, as are the Daltons. The third house is owned by the Rodgers, a two story council house. We get two small jugs of milk each day, for which we pay the Rooneys four pence when we have it. Other times, Daddy does work for them in the forge to pay for it. We aren't allowed to drink the milk because Mammy says it's for tea and stirabout only. But on the rare occasion when we get to, it's great.

It is during one of those roughhouse kicking mule games that I come to mild grief. I can't remember whether I fell out of bed or was kicked out, but I remember lying under the bed crying from the pain in my tummy. I can see the red horsehairs of the mattress poking through the broken springs. The black topcoat we put there to cover the hole in the mattress is nearly touching the floor.

Mammy comes in and asks, "What happened and what have yis done to him now?"

"We did nothing, Mammy," Seán says. "He was just leaning out of the bed and he fell."

She picks me up and calls for Daddy.

Hospital Visit

We're in the hallway of a large white building with a row of windows on one side and doors on the other. Mammy hands me over to a woman in a white dress, wearing a big white hat on her head. I struggle to get back to Mammy, but the woman is too strong for me. I try saying, "Bring me home," but it comes out in a whimper, "Bing e home! Bing e home!"

She asks Mammy, "What's his name?"

Mammy says, "It's Pat."

"Well now, Pat, aren't you the fine big lad? Would you like some sweets? I have lots of sweets in that room." The woman points to a green door.

I don't know whether to continue to struggle or nod, but she takes it as a nod anyways. Then she says to Mammy, "Don't you worry, Mrs. Burke, sure we'll only keep him in a few days and won't we take good care of him?"

Mammy says, "Thank you, Nurse," and walks away.

I don't remember much about that hospital other than rows of beds filled with old men who were always coughing. I remember green and white-painted walls in the hallway and cream-colored walls in the ward. I remember I had more than one blanket and slept in an iron bed, on a mattress with no holes.

I also remember being lonely without brothers and sisters.

But, most of all, I remember the embarrassment as doctors and nurses continually looked at my naked body. After all, I was only three years old.

A Visit to the Doctor

Shortly after my stay in hospital, I am sitting on the bar of the bike so Daddy can take me to the doctor. It has stopped raining and the sun is out. Large potholes filled with water make the sand and gravel road a mine field. Daddy weaves the bike in and out, trying to avoid the bumps. I can smell his stale breath as he struggles to push the bike. His unshaven face brushes mine on either side as he goes up and down from the effort.

Sometimes the front wheel goes into a pothole and I nearly fall off from the jolt. I grip the handlebars with all my might as the rolled up flour sack I'm sitting on slips out from under me. It looks to be a long way down to the road, and I think that if I fall off, the back wheel will run over me and I'll be dead for sure.

Daddy tells me to keep my feet away from the spokes, because he says he doesn't want me to lose some of my toes, on top of everything else. I'm so busy trying to hold on that I nearly forget the other pain.

When we reach the bottom of a big hill, Daddy lifts me off and we walk to the top where he stops to smoke his pipe. After awhile we start off again. At the doctor's house, we enter a room with several chairs and a black fireplace. There is no fire lit in it. A large looking glass hangs over the fireplace, and sitting on the mantelpiece are two little black terrier vases holding withered flowers.

A woman in one of the chairs asks Daddy if I'm the youngest. He says, "No, there's one younger. I have ten at home, two in England regretfully, and Dolly is staying at Colonel Winters in Mearscourt. "

Then she says, looking at me, "I don't know about the others, Joe, but that one is a picture of yourself, a real spark off the anvil. Aren't you a great man, Joe Burke, to be able to feed and clothe all of them."

Before he can answer, a door opens and a man with thick red-rimmed glasses says, "Come in, Joe." We follow him into a room that has what looks like a tall leather bench with a place for resting your feet. Under the window is a table covered by a white cloth, holding a shiny metal tray. A roll of cotton wool and a small container with a lid on it sit beside the tray. Along the walls are white shelves holding bottles and jars of different medicines.

"Well, Joe," he says, "and how is the little fellow today?"

"He seems to be good, but a little sore, Doctor," Daddy says.

The doctor says, "I see. Well, let's have a look."

Daddy picks me up and they unbutton my britches. I feel embarrassed as the doctor examines me, and it's like the hospital all over again. Then he says, "It is a little red." He takes a small jar of ointment from the shelf and puts some of it on me. He tells Daddy, "Have the missus put a little of it on twice a day and he'll be fine."

Daddy thanks him and we leave. When we get back home, Chris starts to shout from the gate, "Bing e home is back. Bing e home is back." My face is red as a beetroot and not for the first time either— they would tease me with that name for many years to come.

When we get in the house, Mammy is cutting slices off a cake of bread. She holds the cake against her apron with her left hand around the outer edge, and then pulls the knife across the top in a sawing motion. When the knife gets in too close to her chest she breaks off the last piece with her thumb. Margaret, Teresa, Chris, Anne and Frank stand by, waiting for their slices, and I join the line. She cuts off six slices and puts jam on them. By the time she makes tea for Daddy we're all waiting for more. She starts cutting again and the cake gets smaller. She says, "I declare, yis won't be happy till it's all gone, and I know it's the jam that's making yis eat."

Daddy starts to tell her about our visit to the doctor and I go outside because I don't want to hear about it. I don't want to go through that embarrassment again. Mammy later told me that I'd had been circumcised. At the time, I didn't know what that big word meant, I knew I just wanted to forget about it.

A few years later when I was in school, a girl asked our teacher, Mrs. O'Kelly, what it meant to be circumcised. We were studying the Bible. Mrs. O'Kelly appeared to be gobsmacked by the question and after a nervous look and a long pause said, "It means to be chosen, child, now no more questions." I remember thinking to myself, well, I hope I'm not bloody well chosen again.

School

Nothing much really happened for the rest of the year in our house. The biggest event was Mammy and Margaret trying to get Teresa ready for her First Holy Communion and Margaret calling her a dunce. Christmas comes and goes, and Santie Claus was stingy. Teresa and Anne got small plastic naked dolls and Margaret got a couple of books. Chris got a flogging top, and Frank and I got a peggy's leg each. I loved eating that small stick of golden brown candy. But try as I might to make it last, it disappeared in no time.

January came, followed by February and March, and then a fat, white-haired woman came to the door. Anne says, "It's Mrs.O'Kelly, the school principal. She came to ask Mammy if she'll let you go to school."

Mammy tells her, "Oh! I don't know if I should. Sure he won't be four years old till next month."

The white-haired woman says, "He may be only four, Mrs. Burke, but he's a fine big lad, and he'd be well able for it. He'd be playing with children close to his own age, and wouldn't he be out from under your feet and you having so much to do? And of course you know that if we haven't got a certain number of children we could lose our second teacher."

On hearing this, I'm showing off for her, running in and out of the house, jumping over Mammy's daffodils. I want to show them I can run and jump as good as Anne, who's already in school. They talk for another while, and then Mammy agrees to let me go. I'm real happy about it and I look forward to tomorrow.

My first day at school is all fun and play, with my sisters showing me off, and I get lots of piggybacks from bigger children. The school consists of one big room with a fireplace in the center of the back wall and a blackboard on each side of the fireplace. A map of the world hangs on the end wall, with a notice board beside it. The back area to the right of the fireplace is called the dunce's corner. When someone doesn't know their lesson, the teacher makes them stand there.

Between the two windows at the front of the room, there's a picture of the Sacred Heart of Jesus with a little red oil lamp below it. I've seen that same picture and lamp in all the village houses I've been in.

A small open space opposite the fireplace separates the schoolroom into two sections. The older children's area has six square wooden tables in two rows, with a bench on either side of the tables. The area near the entrance door at the opposite end has five tables with benches for the smaller children up to fourth class. Both teachers, Mrs. O'Kelly and Mrs. Ward, share a desk in front of the fire.

I'm told the lower classes were taught downstairs until it became too dangerous. The ceiling plaster kept falling down and they had to move everyone upstairs. All the tables have ink stains on them and are worn from many years of use. The boards on the tables have separated from one another and we can see our feet through them when we sit down.

The floorboards have shrunk and separated much like the table boards—some are loose at the joints. These have been circled with chalk and we're told not to walk on them. When the older children sweep up after school, most of the dirt falls down between the boards.

Plaster has dropped off the walls leaving holes behind. There's no ceiling above us, and we can count the rows of slates on the roof.

Where the slates are missing, we can see the sky. A new school is being built near our house, and the bigger children say it's nearly ready.

A gravel path through the playground leads to the lavatory—a small building with a rusty iron roof. Inside is a long bench with two holes in it, one big and one small. For toilet paper we use squares of newspaper from a nearby shelf. The children bring those each day. I heard one of the bigger boys say the teacher knows which houses read the newspaper by those who bring in the paper. A small stream runs along the back of the school. George Scally says there are fish in it. He lives on the main road up past Baltakin crossroads and is eight months older than me.

A tree in front of the lavatory has a place in it where children sit and play a game called "witch in the well." The one who's sitting in the tree plays the witch. All the children get as close to the witch as they dare and ask her, "What do you want?"

"I want a needle and thread."

"What do you want the needle and thread for?"

"To sew a bag."

"What do you want the bag for?"

"To carry sand."

"What do you want the sand for?"

"To sharpen a knife."

"What do you want the knife for?"

"To cut your throat."

At this point the witch jumps out and chases everyone. The children run in all directions, screaming, and if she catches one of them before they reach a certain point, that person becomes the witch. They won't let me play because I'm too small.

On my fourth day of school I get my first slap with the stick across my hand for talking. My thumb swells up and turns black, and I don't like school anymore. Some of the bigger children get slapped all the time, mostly the boys, and some of them cry.

I want to go to the lavatory, but I have to ask in Irish and I don't know how. I stand up and raise my hand, but when the teacher looks at me I can't say anything because I don't know the words. She tells me to sit down and she's real cross. I'm scared of her. I sit down for what seems a very long time, but I have to go, and then it starts to happen.

A bigger kid stands up, and says, "Please, ma'am, Pat Burke has to go to the lavatory."

Mrs. O'Kelly looks at me and the shite is running all down my legs. She tells my sister Margaret, "Take your brother outside and take care of him."

We get to the stream and Margaret stands me in it while she goes in the lavatory for paper. My feet are freezing and my legs are nearly blue from the cold water. Margaret comes back after what seems like a lifetime, saying the paper's all gone. She calls me a dirty little pig and and asks why do I have to shame her before the whole school? She wipes me with grass, but it only spreads the shite more. Then she dips my britches in the water and washes me off with it. Now I'm all wet and my britches are wet too. She wrings them out and takes me back in to school. I don't know how long I sit there till the shivers start.

Someone stands up and says, "Please, ma'am, Pat Burke is shivering."

This time she tells Margaret to take me home. That's my last day at school for a long time, because mostly I'm at home sick.

Chapter Three

A Baby Brother

Mammy is, as she says, "not well in bed," so Margaret and Teresa have to do the cooking.

The way I see it, there isn't much cooking to do—just boil the potatoes and cabbage. Daddy comes home with a steak to fry for himself and smells of drink. He eats and goes up to sleep in the box room. I've never seen him do that before, as he always sleeps in the same bed as Mammy. Frank goes around the house with no britches on and his legs all covered with shite. He tries to climb up on Mammy's bed and she shouts down, "Is there no one to take care of that child? I declare yis are a useless lot of articles."

Teresa takes him outside to the barrel of water to clean him up. She does a lot of mumbling to herself. The only thing I can make out is her saying is "I'll never have a baby."

Anne wants to know where they will sleep now that Daddy has taken their bed. Margaret says, "I don't know. Maybe in the same place baby Jesus slept."

Then she tells Anne, "You can go in with Pat and Chris for the night. Teresa and I will wait till Daddy gets up."

Anne says, "How can four of us fit in one bed?"

Margaret tells her, "Seán is staying the night with Mick Brennan so there'll only be the three of you."

Mammy shouts down for someone to close the door, as she wants to get some sleep. Mrs. Geraghty, a neighbor, is up in the room with Mammy. A woman I've never seen before comes to the door with a black bag and goes up to the room. She keeps going in and out. I found out later that she was the midwife. The woman tells Mammy, "It won't be long now." Then she tells Mrs. Geraghty to get our father up. Chris, Anne, Margaret, Teresa and I are sent off to bed. At some strange hour of the night I can hear a baby crying and I don't know what's going on. I wonder why someone would bring a baby to our house at this time of night.

Then I think maybe it's the Banshee (ghostly woman who foretells death), because they're supposed to wail like a baby. But I remember hearing Mrs. Crinegan say the Banshee can only be heard when someone is going to die. Then I wonder if Chris and Anne heard it too. Maybe one of them is dead. I give them a little kick and they move, so I know it's not them. I know I don't want it to be me, and it can't be Tom, Watt, or Joe in the big bed—they're too big to die, and besides I can hear them breathing and snorting like pigs.

I still can't go to sleep because there's a mouse in the room and it keeps making noises. It seems to be tearing at a piece of the wallpaper, making enough racket to wake the dead. We never hear them during the day. I want to go outside and pee, but I'm scared of the mouse and the Banshee.

After God's own amount of time I fall asleep, and the next thing I know I'm the only one left in bed. Down in the kitchen, Margaret gives me tea in a panny with a slice of bread. Daddy sends her to get Dolly. She meets Dolly on her way home from Mearscourt, and Dolly puts her on the carrier of the bike 'til they get to the gate. Dolly rushes straight up to Mammy's bedroom closing the door behind her.

Daddy, Tom, Joe, and Watt have gone off to work, and Teresa sits by the fire drinking tea. No one seems worried about going to school.

Teresa and Anne look all tired and their hair isn't even combed. Chris says, "They look like something a cat would drag in on frosty morning." Mammy's door is still closed. Margaret opens it, peeks in, and asks, "Are yis okay? Can we come in now?"

We all go inside to find a little baby wrapped in a woolly blanket lying beside Mammy. She tells us, "This is your little baby brother." Then for some reason I don't understand, she starts to cry. It makes me feel all strange and funny inside, because I've never seen her cry before.

Then, we're all over the baby, and I get to hold his hand. It's no bigger than a doll's hand. He has a small round head with very little hair on it.

Everyone has an opinion as to who he looks like and what color his hair will be. Dolly says, "Sure he's the spitting image of Daddy. Just look at his eyes and mouth. If that's not Daddy's head, I'll eat my hat." I wonder if Daddy has no head now.

Later, Seán comes home, and he says, "Ah, God, he's grand." Then he blurts out, "Mammy, Mammy, but where did yis get him?" Mammy looks at him in a strange sort of way, and she makes eyes at Dolly. Then she smiles and says, "I bought him in Mullingar." I wonder how she could have done that and she in bed for several days.

Dolly says to him, "You bloody eejit. Where do you think we got him? Under a head of cabbage?"

Later I heard Dolly saying to Margaret, "Isn't Seán a thick lug? How is it that he doesn't even know where babies come from, and he nearly fourteen years of age?" Margaret just listened, probably because she didn't know where babies came from either.

I don't believe that Mammy got the baby under a head of cabbage, because Anne and I often looked in the garden and there was never a baby there. Then I think maybe the woman who kept going in and out of the room brought him. I tell Teresa what I'm thinking.

Teresa says, "That's it, she must have had him in the black bag."

Margaret said, "The bag must've a hole in it so the baby could breathe."

It was a strange day, that June 10, 1942, the day the last Burke was born in Moyvore, my youngest brother, Eddie.

Household Smells and Stuff

There are a lot of different smells in our house, what with the chimney always smoking and the smell of burning turf and sticks mixed with the scent of boiling cabbage and fried bacon. Boiling cabbage has a strong smell, especially when it's green. That, plus the smell from the pot in Mammy and Daddy's room, mixed with Jeyes fluid is enough to make you sick.

Joe says, "It's the boiling snails in the cabbage that puts the bad smell in the house." Mammy tells him to go and wash his mouth out with Jeyes fluid. We use the Jeyes fluid to disinfect the kitchen floor when we wash it out on Fridays. It's a black disinfectant that turns white when mixed with water.

Mammy put camphor balls in the trunk so the moths wouldn't eat the clothes and Tom's ironed shirt. Frank finds one of them and thinks it's a sweet. He spends the next several minutes on his belly on Mammy's lap, while she pounds on his back for him to spit it up. She speaks to the house. "Glory be ta God what won't yis get up to next? Can't any of yis look after that child when yis see I'm busy with the baby?"

Mostly Frank is potty trained and the only one allowed to use the pot in Mammy and Daddy's room. Once in awhile he does a big load in his britches and tries to climb up on her lap. Usually she's busy with Eddie and pushes him away.

When the three-legged pot isn't boiling food, it's boiling clothes, including dirty nappies. We had a second pot for that, but it got cracked and leaked all over the place. There's a hollow area in the cement floor in front of the fireplace, and sometimes we team the water from the pot of potatoes there. Then we use a scrubbing brush and a burlap sack to clean that part of the floor. This doesn't happen often, as Mammy likes to keep the floor dry during the week. Of course, keeping the floor dry doesn't happen very often either, with everyone going in and out.

Most of the time Mammy feeds Eddie at the fire. She puts a big jumper across her shoulder and hides him under it. I don't know what she's doing, but when I try to look she pushes me away. I can't understand why she has to hide Eddie while feeding him.

When she finishes whatever it is she's doing, she lays a newspaper on the floor in front of the fireplace, takes off his nappy, and holds him between her knees close to the fire. She says, "Come on now, be a good lad and do a pee pee on the fire. Atta good boy! Pee pee on the fire for Mammy." She says it in a kind of a singsongy lilt, like when she gives out the rosary. Soon it comes out of his spout in an arc, making sparks and ashes go up the chimney.

Margaret tells her, "It's no wonder the poor little divil pees, and the arse nearly burning off him."

Mammy waits another while to see if anything falls on the newspaper. If it does, she wraps it up and throws it in the fire. She takes a three-cornered nappy, once white, but now dark gray from too many boilings, and puts it under him. She shakes lots of Johnson and Johnson's powder on him and rubs his arse like she does when she's making a cake of bread. She turns him over on his back, pins the diaper together, and he's ready for his nap.

A Scourge: Nits and Lice

For some reason, we always have lice in our house. We call them bindies. They're small yellow bugs and they get into our hair and clothes. Mammy shakes DDT in the beds to get rid of them, and it smells bad. It's a white powder that comes in a round tin with holes in the top. Seán says it's worse than poison, and he'd rather suffer being eaten by the bindies.

The mattress in our bed has a big hole in it, and the boards are showing. Tom put the boards across it after we fell through the spring several times. Seán says the mattress is all rotted away from me pissing in the bed. I call him a liar and he hits me a good one.

Mammy puts a topcoat over the hole and covers it with a sheet. Seán says he slept in a bed in Mullingar one time and there was two sheets on the bed. I wonder why they had two sheets—maybe they didn't have enough blankets. We use two blankets and a topcoat over us. I'm the smallest, so I have to go to bed first. I don't like that, because when Seán and Chris come to bed they're all cold and they stick their feet in my belly to warm themselves. Then they pull the blankets up over my head and I nearly choke from the smell of DDT. Sometimes I go outside for a pee and by the time I get back in bed I'm freezing, and they get real vexed.

When Daddy stays home some evenings, he sits at the fire and helps to get rid of the bindies. He pulls them off with his fingers and drops them into the fire. He puts his hand down my back where I'm itching, finds one, and throws it on the fire. It makes a popping sound.

Each night Mammy gives out the Rosary. We all kneel in a half circle with our backs to the fire. Small stones stick out of the cement floor where we chop the firewood, and they hurt my knees. The logs explode sometimes and hot cinders fly out onto our legs. Seán doesn't care, because he has long britches. A big cinder lands on my leg and I'm trying to get it off without losing the lilt of the prayer: "Thou O Lord wilth open my lips, and my tongue shall announce thy praise. Incline onto my aid, O God. O Lord, make haste to help me."

Just then Seán whispers to Chris, "And God get the hot cinders off Pat's legs."

Chris bursts out laughing and Daddy gives him a beating for his troubles when we finish.

No Britches

It's nearly time for school and I can't find my britches. All of us have looked for them. I'm glad my shirt's too long for me and goes down to my knees.

Anne asks me, "What do you need a britches for, won't you do the way you are? Now all you have to do is put on my jumper and won't everyone think you are a girl. Sure you can sit in the girl's class and play in our playground."

I tell her, "I'll kill you, you long-haired maggot."

I know she only says things like that to get me vexed. Teresa says I'm worse for listening to her. One time, Chris put maggots in the pocket of her blouse, and she blamed me for it. When Mammy went to go wash it, she found the maggots in the pocket and gave Anne a good telling off. That's when we nicknamed her the Maggot. Now anytime we want to get her vexed, we call her that.

Seán is nowhere to be seen. We think he left the house early by getting out the window again. He's been doing that ever since Mrs. O'Kelly gave him four slaps for telling her she was doing a sum wrong. It turned out later he was right. That was two weeks ago. She came to our house and asked Mammy to send him back to school, as he was one of her better pupils. When Seán heard it, he said that Mrs. O'Kelly couldn't care less whether he was good or bad—all she wanted was to keep the school attendance up.

He said to Chris, "There will be white blackbirds lost in snow before I go back to that school again."

So, Daddy hid Seán's britches last night, and now mine are gone. They're the same color and made from the same bolt of cloth. Mammy says Seán couldn't have mistaken them, because his legs are long and mine are short, and even if he did take them, how in God's own name could he get into them?

Teresa says, "Where there's a will there's a way."

He comes home every day when school is nearly out, and Mammy feeds him. She tries to get him to tell her where he goes, but all he says is he has his own little house in a secret place, and he'd stay there all the time only it gets too cold at night. We all know it's just down the fields, but still no one can find him.

Mrs. Crinegan says to Mammy, "It isn't right for a young lad to be that scared of school, and he shouldn't be forced to go back." Then she says, "I have an extra bed at my house and there's a lot of work needed to be done around the place. I can't pay him much, but sure wouldn't it it be a roof over his head and do him till he gets something better?"

Mrs. Crinegan has a small farm down the Chapel Road that was left to her by an uncle. She comes to our house a lot, and herself and Mammy talk over tea. She tells ghost stories and sometimes, after listening to her, I lay awake in bed thinking I can see a green man with a pointed nose and red eyes and a pitchfork ready to get me. The only way I can stop seeing him is to cover my head with the blanket.

Later on Mammy tells Daddy what Mrs. Crinegan said, and he agrees that Seán should quit school. But then he says, "Seán will not go to work for that auld gossip." He tells Mammy that there's a position open for a shop boy in Limerick and Seán can do his apprenticeship there.

Before he leaves for Limerick, Seán takes me down to see his hiding place. It's a huge stump of a tree in a ditch and is covered over with bushes and nettles. He hollowed out the inside of the tree and crawled up inside it. He couldn't be seen even by those standing right beside it. I'm delighted to inherit it.

Mammy gives him back his britches and I get mine back also. Two days later, Seán is on his way to Martins' of Doon, County Limerick, to serve his time as an apprentice shopkeeper.

The Loft

A big shed sits between our forge and Shaw's pub; we call it Kenny's shed. It's a long building with a galvanized roof, with the gable end facing the road. The men play handball against it on the weekends. The shed has a loft with hay in one end and a hand mill in the other for separating the chaff from the wheat or oats. Double doors open in the middle of the building, with a steel beam extending above them holding a pulley wheel and a rope.

Anthony Tormey who's three years older than me says the pulley is for hauling up bales of sheep wool and grain. There's one like it in the yard behind Shaw's pub, and he says that one is used to weigh drunken men. I don't believe him. Jimmy McQuaid, who's my age and a son of the manager in Shaw's says that's a lie, because he lives there and he never saw anyone weigh themselves.

The rope is tied to a ring in the wall where only the bigger boys can reach it. Sometimes they use it as a swing and pull one another up and down. When they do this, one has to be on the lookout for Gus Kenny, the local butcher, who's very cross. We'd be in trouble for sure if he caught us playing in the shed.

The Kennys lived next door to us in our old house in the village. Gus has a car and always has trouble starting it. One time he skinned his knuckles while fixing a puncture and in a fit of temper made a big dinge in the car with a hammer.

When the car isn't parked at the butcher shop, we know it's safe to play in the loft. The only way up to it is by a ladder fixed to the back wall that goes up through a small trap door. Jimmy and me are barely able to climb it. One end of the shed holds cattle to be killed for the butcher shop. The other end is for the car in the winter, and the middle is used to hold turf, the ass' cart, and wheelbarrows for the bog.

Sometimes the Kenny children play with us, but they're real sissies and when they don't get their own way, they threaten to tell their parents on us, and then we have to leave. One day we're all playing hide and seek and I find I'm the only one left in the loft. Just before I climb down the ladder, I hear a noise up in the hay. I climb up and Liam Tormey calls me over to the dark corner. He's fifteen. He puts my hand on his private part sticking out of his britches and asks me if I had ever seen one so big. Then he says, "Do you know Paidin, that if you ride a woman you would get a baby?"

I don't know anything about that, but I do know people don't go around with their hands on other people's private parts. They might hold hands, and once I saw Daddy kissing Mammy, but I never saw anyone do that. When he lets go of my hand, I get out of there in a hurry—and it's the fastest I ever climbed down that ladder.

One week later I'm behind the goalposts in Garrison's field where Moyvore is playing Milltown in a football match. Lilly Rodgers is on her hands and knees giving me a horsey ride. She goes a short way and I fall off, which means it's the next kid's turn. We have great fun, but I can't understand how I can get a baby by doing it.

35

PATRICK BURKE

Home Schooling

I'm preparing for my first Holy Communion and Mammy is going over my lesson for the next day. She says to me, "You can remember anything when you have a mind to." Daddy is sitting on the table with his back to the wall beside the rear window, reading the newspaper. He reads the newspaper every day and sometimes calls on one of us to read it to him. It's his way of finding out if we're learning what we're supposed to in school. When we get stuck and can't say the words, he starts on about the poor quality of teaching in the school.

Just over his head, the paraffin oil lamp hangs from a nail in the wall. The globe is all black on one side where he lights pieces of paper from it to light his pipe. He smokes a crooked pipe with a plug tobacco called Bendigo. It comes in a small dark brown bar wrapped in yellow paper. He cuts it with his penknife and rubs it between his hands to make it ready for the pipe. Mammy thinks he gets more pleasure from getting it ready and trying to light it than he does from actually smoking it.

He has his two feet up on the table and they're as high as his shoulders. The newspaper lies across his knees. I'm looking all around the room pretending I'm not listening to what Mammy reads to me. Daddy looks over the top of the paper at me and I know he's ready to give me a beating if I make a mistake. He jumps down from the table and stands over me ready to take off his belt.

"Now Breenie," he says, "you ask him those questions." He always calls her Breenie.

Mammy asks me the questions and I answer every one of them. "Now, Joe," she says, "wasn't he listening and doesn't he know all of them?"

Daddy grabs his topcoat off the nail behind the door. She asks him where he is going and he says he's going down to lock up the forge.

"Why do you have to go down? Can't one of the young ones do it?"

He says, "Maybe they could, but there are some things a man has

36

to do for himself." With that he opens the door and walks into the night.

After he leaves, Anne says to me, "You done that on purpose and the next time he'll lay the leather belt on you anyway."

A World Champion

Daddy is on his knees with his fists up, saying he's the world-boxing champion and I'm the challenger. Chris acts as the referee and tells us to start fighting on the count of three. I make fists and try to hit him, but his arms and fists are too big and get in the way. He sticks out his tongue at me and I hit him on the arms and elbows. I hurt my hands and I'm nearly in tears.

When he drops his arms and turns to talk to Mammy, I hit him on the chin, and he falls down on his back and lies there with his eyes closed. Mammy exclaims, "My God you've knocked out the world champion!"

I wonder is he hurt, but then I think he's only playing. I move closer to take a look to be sure and he wakes up with a laugh and grabs me. He tickles me real good and finishes it off with a rub of the beard. I don't like it when he does that, because it makes my face all red and his breath smells from the porter and the pipe.

Chris and I then take a turn fighting. When I hit his nose, he runs away crying. Mammy says, "Joe, I do wish you wouldn't have them fighting each other."

Daddy tells me, "Well done." I don't like hitting Chris like that. Besides, he's older than me and will beat me up later.

Now that Seán has left, we have more room in the bed. Even better, I don't have his feet in my face all the time. Frank is in with us now, but he's small and doesn't take up much room. Joe is always snoring and Watt regularly gives him a good pinch. He then roars like a bull and they start fighting. Tom shouts at them to be quiet, because morning comes soon enough.

Watt is working for Arthur Mearse, a big farmer, and Joe works for the land commission. We have lots of food in the house and Teresa says it's a bloody miracle.

Joe and Daddy don't get along well at all these days because Daddy wants him to give up more of his wages on Friday. Joe says he won't do it.

It's Friday again and they are standing shoulder to shoulder in the middle of the kitchen. Watt is trying to separate them. Daddy grabs the tongs and prepares to hit Joe with it. Mammy cries out, "No Joe, not with the tongs." Daddy drops the tongs and then grabs a piece of fire wood and hits Joe over the head with it. Joe falls to the floor and there is blood running down his face. Mammy shouts, "My God, Joe, you've killed him."

After a while, Joe gets to his feet and starts to leave. As he's going out the door, Daddy shouts after him, "And don't you ever come near this house again." When Daddy leaves later on to go to the forge, Mammy says to Watt, "Your father gets more miserable and cantankerous by the day, and you brother Joe is like a wounded weasel."

That evening, Joe went to live with Donald Rush, a small farmer down past the village.

Catechism

The priest is in school to examine us for our First Holy Communion. He asks each of us five questions, and just two of us get all five right. He asks me what would happen if I went to confession with two sins and only told one of them.

I respond, "I would have three sins coming out, Father."

He has a smile on his face and asks me to explain.

I say, "Because it is a sin to make a bad confession, Father."

"That's right," he says, "and because you withheld one it means you don't get forgiveness for the two, plus you add another for holding one back. That is very good, very good."

We get the rest of the day off school because the teacher has to serve tea and sweet cake to the priest.

When Daddy heard about my answer to the priest's question, he laughed out loud. For days after, he could be heard telling anyone who would listen that Pat went to confession with two sins and came away with three.

The Bus

Mammy and I are at the crossroads waiting for the bus to Mullingar town, where we'll buy my First Communion clothes. The bus comes from Ballymahon, which is six miles away from Moyvore. It's another twelve miles to Mullingar. I've never been on a bus before and I'm really looking forward to it.

The owner and driver of the bus is called the Tit Naton. I don't know why he's called that. Mammy says he owns a garage and petrol pumps in Ballymahon.

The insides of my legs above my knees are all red and chaffed from the wind. I'm wearing Anne's jumper because mine is all black and shiny from the elbow to the wrist. It got that way from rubbing it across my nose all the time. Watt says I always have candles hanging out of my nose. Now they call me "snotty nose," "candles," and "bing e home." I don't like wearing a girl's jumper because they'll probably call me a sissy too. I have enough names as it is.

A woman comes over to Mammy and asks if she is going on the bus and would she buy her a shirt in Mullingar? She said she left her husband's shirt out on the bushes to dry, and when she got up this morning the goats had eaten it. Then she says, "You know, Mrs. Burke, that Ned will kill me if he hasn't got a shirt for Mass."

Mammy tells her she's only too willing to get her a shirt and asks, "And what size would you like, missus?"

The woman says the size isn't important just so long as it is a man's shirt and made from flannel. She hands a ten shilling note to

Mammy and says, "The blessings of God on you, Mrs. Burke. I'll be waiting right here this evening for the bus."

When the bus finally arrives, it is red and white, with red leather seats inside. We go to the back and I climb on the last seat which is like a bench. I can slide from one side of the bus to the other along the seat, and by getting up on my knees I can see out the back window. A man in the next seat tells me that the space under that seat is for holding the spare wheel and tools in case the bus breaks down. I'm almost hoping we break down so I can see how all those things fit under the seat.

There are seven or eight people on the bus, all carrying shopping bags. A woman with a straw hat tells Mammy that the bus will be full by the time we get to Mullingar. She explains, "It used to run twice a week, but now it only goes on fair days, and wouldn't you know that's the worst time for bargains. Ah well, the shopkeepers love it, sure isn't it more money in their pockets, and they never seem to have enough."

The windows of the bus shake and rattle when the wheels go in the potholes, and I wonder if they ever fall out. We pick up more people at the hill of Skeagh near Garrison's field, where the men play football. Halfway up the hill, the bus really slows down and black smoke pours out the back. I think to myself that I could run as fast as the bus. We pass a horse and cart and I can look down on them. I wonder—if our house had wheels would it be much bigger than the bus? When we get to the top of the hill I look back down and it must be over a mile to the bottom. The bus moves quickly down the other side of the hill and I think we must be doing a hundred miles an hour.

Liam Mahon who is in my class told me that they have cars in America that can do over a hundred miles an hour, and that's the speed of sound. He says it's no lie, because he has a cousin in Boston who told him.

I hear one woman telling another that the county council is going to take the top off the hill of Skeagh because the lorries hauling turf from Bord Na Móna to Dublin can't get up it with a full load. Now they have to go around Milltown to bypass the hill. I am dying to ask how they can take the top off a hill.

40

It's great to look down on the cattle and sheep grazing in the fields. Tomorrow, I can tell them at school that I went to Mullingar on the bus. Anthony Tormey said he used to get on the bus all the time when it stopped in Moyvore in the evenings. He used to watch it for the driver, while the driver stopped in the pub. That driver doesn't drive it any more and the bus no longer stops there.

We come to one part of the road where tree tops grow over the land from each side and meet at the top, making a leafy tunnel. It looks like the top of the bus nearly touches the trees.

Soon after, we come to the bridge of Shandonagh, and the bus seems bigger than the entire bridge. Mammy whispers to me, "This is supposed to be the most dangerous bridge in all of Ireland." A car on the other side waits for us to go over first. I think maybe I want to be a bus driver when I get big. They must be special people.

Shopping

Mullingar town is crowded with people gathered in front of the shops, and cattle standing in the middle of the Main Street. Cow dung is scattered all over the street and the footpaths. Our bus slows down while people move the cattle so we can pass.

I have never seen so many shops before—there must be nearly fifty of them. The glass in the windows of some of the shops is nearly half the size of the bus. The bus finally comes to a stop up in front of a pub and everyone piles out to go shopping.

Near the pub, I watch as a man spits on his hand, hits another man's hand and says, "That's my last offer, take it or leave it." When the second man doesn't respond, the first turns to walk away, but then a third man pulls him back and talks to the two men. The first man spits on his hand again and hits the other again, and then they shake hands. Mammy tells me they would argue over a penny. I ask her why they hit each other and she says, "It's called making a bargain." I don't know what a bargain is, but it must be something to do with hitting.

We go in and out of several shops, some with sawdust on the floors. The floors are all wet from the rain and cow dung. Some shopkeepers are outside sweeping with yard brushes. All the shops have electric lights dangling from the ceilings. I am amazed that the lights turn on with a switch on the wall. The two pubs in Moyvore have gaslights that have to be lit with a match.

Inside one shop, Mammy asks for a two-penny ice cream. The man takes the lid off a steel box that has frost on the inside. He takes out what looks like a two-pound bar of white butter and cuts a thick slice off it. He puts it between two biscuits and hands it to Mammy. She gives it to me and tells me to eat slowly and enjoy it. I'm not sure what it is, but I go outside and take a big bite out of it. The pain shoots through my teeth almost instantly, and when I can't stand it anymore I spit it out and throw the rest against the shop railing.

We go to another shop where Mammy buys a bolt of cloth. She says the ready-made clothes are too dear, and she will have Lack Scott, the tailor, make a suit for Chris and me. I have to remember not to wipe my nose on Anne's sleeve. Before we left the house, Mammy gave me a handkerchief she tore from an old sheet and told me to be sure and use it.

After buying the cloth, we head back to the bus. When we arrive, we're told it won't be leaving for about half an hour.

Just then a man walks up and shakes hands with Mammy saying, "Mrs. Burke, I declare I haven't seen you in ages. Won't you join me for a drink?"

She says, "Ah no, I shouldn't."

He tells her there is a little snug in the back of the pub where we won't be seen. We go into the pub and she says she'll have a glass of port wine. He gets her the wine and he gives me a glass of red lemonade, which I drink down, glad it isn't ice cream. As they're talking, I get to thinking about that ice cream. I remember it tasted really good. I run outside and up the street to the place where I threw it, but it's gone. I wonder if a dog got it or was there another boy shopping for his First Communion clothes who took it.

When I get back to the bus, people are getting on for the trip home. Mammy is all smiling and happy, and that makes me feel good.

Chapter Four

Devil or Saint?

"You're either a devil or a saint. From the day we're born, we're in training to be one or the other. What do you think, Father Daly?"

"Well, you may have a point there, Joe, but the way we live our lives determines what we are or what we become."

"Then it would be a safe bet to assume there are already a lot of devils in Ireland."

Father Daly laughs and says, "There's a lot of good and bad in all of us, Joe."

"That's right, Father, sure it's all a part of being human. And even Jesus, as great as he was, had his faults; like when he was tempted by the devil."

"Well, Joe! I don't know if they could be called faults."

"Okay then, Father, how about when he lost his temper and drove the traders from the temple?"

"Yes, Joe, he did that, but maybe it was his way of showing the people how something like that should be treated."

"That could be the lesson, Father; it all depends on how one sees things."

"Do you believe in the Bible, Joe?"

"I do. Well, I believe in the New Testament. Now the Old Testament has a lot of strange things in it. We're told God gave man a free will of his own, yet Moses killed three thousand of his own people when they dared to worship a golden calf."

"Yes, Joe, but that was the law of the land in those days."

"I know it was, Father, and it was the law followed by the people in the time of Jesus. Remember he said, 'I have come to uphold the laws not to destroy them.'"

Daddy spent many years studying with the Monks of Clara as a young man and never passed up a chance to discuss religion. I'm sitting in the back seat of Father Daly's car as he drives us to a football match. I can't wait to get there, because it's bad enough to be scared of Daddy, without adding the priest to it. I really think I'm more scared of Daddy.

The older people always say children should be seen and not heard. I know for sure I won't be heard, and if they could read my mind, they'd have me out of this car in no time, and probably give me a beating too. Why couldn't they take Chris or Frank to the football match? Why me? Why should I be the one sitting like a statue in the back seat, afraid to open my mouth? Why should I be the one to keep my dirty feet hanging so I won't stain the red leather seat? Why should I be the one who's too scared to let down the car window with that shiny handle with the round ball on the end of it? Why do I have to be Daddy's favorite when I don't want to be?

The car is filled with smoke from Daddy's pipe, and it burns my eyes. They don't talk to me, just to each other. Daddy asks Father Daly about the marks of Christ on St. Francis, and so another story begins.

We have two priests in Moyvore: Father McManus is the parish priest and Father Daly is the curate. I don't know what a curate is. Anne told me it's one who cures people, but I don't believe her. Both the priests have cars—in fact, all priests have cars. I wonder if I'll ever own a car. I know I'll never be a priest. They're always telling people what to do.

Our two priests live in the parish house with the housekeeper, Mary Gallagher. Her brother Pat ran the farm for the priests till he drank weed killer and died. Mrs. Crinegan said it was because that bitch of a sister of his had him half starved. "Sure himself and herself were always fighting," Pat Shanley told Mammy it was because some girl jilted him, whatever that meant. Himself and my brother

Joe were good friends. Joe was very upset about it. The two of them were talking at the Belfry on Sunday where Pat had just rung the bell for the Angelus, and a few hours later he was dead. Joe could hardly believe it.

First Mass is always said in Moyvore on Sundays. Most people go to where Father Daly says Mass, because he isn't as cross as Father McManus, who's white haired with a bad temper. He's always preaching about the fires of hell and telling people that's where they're headed if they don't change their ways. He also says there's another war coming and he can hear the bombs falling in his ears.

People don't like going to confession to him either, because he gives too much penance. Anne tells me she hates going to confession to him because of all the questions he asks her.

"Do you play with boys?"

"Yes, Father, we play games."

"And what sort of games do ye play?"

"We play leap frog, Father."

"I see, and where do you play these games?"

"In Mearse's field, Father."

"And do the boys do anything else when you play with them?"

"Yes, Father, they pull my dress up over my head and run away, Father."

"Then what do you do?"

" I run after them with a stick, Father."

"And do ye do anything else?"

"No, Father."

"Now, my child, don't be afraid to tell me, who are those boys?"

"My three brothers, Father.

"Oh, I see, well for your penance, say three Hail Mary's."

Daddy and Father McManus don't get along since Daddy did the last job for him and didn't get paid for it. He gave Daddy a whiskey in the parlor, and then asked him why he was so fond of the drink. Daddy told him, "I take a drink to be social and did so with Father Dunne before you came here and I dare you call him a bad man." And so the story was told.

Finally, we arrive at the match and Father Daly and Daddy stop talking. Moyvore wins the match and we're delighted. On the way home, the pair are talking about the marks on St. Francis. They talk non-stop the whole way home. I can't wait to get to our house so I can get out of the car away from them both.

Theft of a Plough

It's September 1946 and we're all back at school. Margaret left for the convent in Ballymahon to begin her second year as a boarder. All in all things are looking up for the Burkes. We have plenty of food in our house and clothes on our backs. Gus Kenny, the butcher, went broke owing a lot of money to the local farmers for cattle. The story appeared in the local paper, and Teresa said, "It's good enough for them with their high and mighty ways, let them put that in their pipe and smoke it. Now maybe they won't be making snide remarks about the Burkes living in a council house."

A lot of whispering goes on in our house and I don't know what's it's about. But, to me, things are looking good overall and we're holding our heads high. Then it happens.

Kathleen Kenny brings a newspaper to school and gives it to Mrs. O'Kelly who has Teresa read it to the class. Teresa begins in a low voice: "Moyvore man fined for theft. At Mullingar district court yesterday, Joe Burke, blacksmith, Moyvore, was fined two pounds for stealing parts of a plough. The plaintiff, a Mr. Michael Higgins, told the court he left in a plough for repairs and Mr. Burke used it for spare parts. When told the defendant was not in court, the judge said he had no choice but to rule in favor of the plaintiff. He ordered Mr. Burke to pay two pounds to Mr. Higgins within ten days."

"Well now," says Mrs. O'Kelly when Teresa finished, "your father must have money to burn that he can afford to send Maggie to boarding school. I hope it stays fine for him. Maybe when he pays his fine it won't be so plentiful."

Teresa comes home crying and tells Mammy what Mrs. O'Kelly said. Sobbing now, Teresa says, "I was never so ashamed in all my life, Mammy. And that bloody auld bitch made me read it out before the whole class. If the nuns hear about this, they'll throw Margaret out of boarding school. Why did he do it, Mammy? Why did he have to steal parts of a lousy auld plough and get our name in the paper?"

Mammy says, "He didn't steal it. That plough was sitting outside the forge for nearly a year and your Daddy didn't even know who it belonged to."

"Well, if that be the case, why then didn't he go to court and fight it?"

"He did go, but he got a puncture this side of Mullingar and he was too late for court."

Teresa says, "A likely story. I'll bet you he wasn't too late for the pub."

Mammy tells her to close her mouth and go and wash the potatoes for dinner.

The next day, Daddy walks into our classroom and Mrs. O'Kelly jumps to her feet. "Joe Burke, how dare you walk into my school without knocking?"

He's carrying his blacksmith's bag in his right hand and I can see the rasp and the pincers sticking out the top. I think he must be on his way somewhere to shoe a horse. He's wearing his new tweed cap, not the old one with the top all black from coal dust. He stands there looking around the classroom as though seeing it for the first time. He looks awfully big as he towers over the room filled with school children. He pushes back the peak of his cap and approaches Mrs. O'Kelly.

"Did you say your school? I understand it belongs to the people of the parish."

"What do you want, and couldn't it have waited till school is out?"

"No, it could not. I want the children to hear what I have to say, just like you let them hear yesterday."

Miss Finnerty, the assistant teacher who followed him in from the other classroom, says, "I don't know what you've been told, Joe Burke, but children do lie."

"Yes, Miss Finnerty, children do lie—and so did your brothers."

"I am certainly not aware of that."

"Well then, if you check Stubbs' Gazette (public record of wrongdoings), you'll find out."

Turning back to Mrs. O'Kelly, he says, "Now I might have money to burn, and if I do, at least I earned it. I didn't steal it like your husband did, Mrs. O'Kelly, when he collected the insurance money."

"I don't know what you're talking about," Mrs. O'Kelly sniffed indignantly.

"Well, then, if you'd ever read Stubbs' Gazette you would have seen it there, too."

Joe Cormack shouts from the back of the classroom, "Good man yourself, Joe Burke, fair play to ya, that's telling her."

All the older boys join in. "Good on you, Joe!"

Mrs. O'Kelly calls for quiet, but they ignore her. She bangs her desk with the metal weight she uses to hold down her papers and shouts, "Class dismissed." At this stage, her face is all red and splotchy. Taking off her glasses, she screams at Daddy, "Get out of my school, Joe Burke! Get out this minute."

We all make a mad dash toward the door, with Daddy in the middle of us all. It's half past one and the end of school for the day. As we rush through the doorway, Teresa says to me, "What more can go wrong? She'll really have it in for us now."

Later that evening, the priest comes to our house and we're put outside while he and Daddy talk. Some of it was repeated to me later.

"Joe, you shouldn't have walked into the school unannounced. And talking to Mrs. O'Kelly like that in front of the children is more than I can tolerate. Now I want you to apologize to Mrs. O'Kelly and give me your promise it will never happen again."

"No, Father, not while there's a single drop of blood in my body will I apologize. Now, maybe I shouldn't have done it. Maybe I shouldn't have said it. But if you had a proper teacher that would stick to teaching and not be sticking her nose in people's private business, then I wouldn't have to. Now if you like, we can take this up with the authorities and maybe they would like to know what's going on in that school."

To my knowledge, Daddy never did apologize, and he did write to the school authorities. Mrs. O'Hara, the postmistress, a good friend of Mammy's, found the letter and asked Mammy not to send it, as it would only make more trouble. Mammy read the letter, took it home, and burned it.

Shoeing Wheels

Shoeing wheels is a big event at our forge and takes place once or twice a year, depending on the number of wheels to be shod.

Outside the forge sits a round slab of cement about seven feet wide, with a round hole in the center about one foot wide. This hole is for the center of the wheel, called the knaft, where the spokes come together. To the right of this slab is the area where the hoops are heated and reddened. On the other side is the water trough we fill from the pump across the road. The pump came about as a result of Daddy starting a petition to the county council requesting and outlining the need for a pump for the people of the village.

We lay large iron hoops on three pieces of iron which are about three inches thick. The hoops have to be off the ground so as to allow the fire to get under them. Smaller hoops are then placed inside the bigger ones. Next, we build two rows of turf around them like bricks, inside and out. They're built up five or six rows, depending on how many wheels are to be shod. Watt and I perform this job while Daddy and Tom work inside the forge. Watt builds the rows while I hand him the sods of turf. When the rows are high enough, we fill the middle with smaller sods and pieces we call clods. That's one of my jobs for the day.

When I finish, Watt takes a sod from the bottom row, inside and out, in four or five places. He then stuffs burning pieces of coal in those spaces to start the fire going. It can take several hours from the time he lights it before the hoops are reddened.

These are good times for me in school. The boys ask me, "When your father is shoeing wheels, can we watch?"

I feel like I'm king of the roost, picking those who can and those who can't watch. I know I don't have the right to tell them they can't watch from across the road, but it's our forge and our fire—and besides, it's great to have power over them. Some even ask me if I'll let them carry water. This way they can get closer to the big fire.

We never know ahead of time if we can shoe because of the weather. Rain will put out the fire. Mrs. Crinegan who has a wireless tells Mammy we're promised good weather. If it comes up raining, Daddy says, "Radio Eireann got it wrong again. Either that or she's lying again." I always want it to rain on a Saturday; that way we'll have to do the shoeing during the week and I get to miss school.

When the fire is going good, I start hauling water to the trough, which is about three feet long, two feet wide, and a foot deep. The bottom is just gravel, so a lot of the water soaks away. I can only manage three quarters of a bucket at a time and I wonder if I'll ever get it filled. But when I think I'd be better off in school, I remember Mrs. O'Kelly and decide I'd rather be hauling water.

Sometimes people from the village complain about the smoke from the fire. They say, "Why can't Joe Burke shoe his wheels when the wind blows away from the village?"

Watt says, "It's too bloody bad about them, and besides it will help prepare some of them for where they're going in the next life."

I finally get the trough filled, along with some cans of water we'll be needing later, and just as I get finished and want to mess around, Daddy sends me home to get tea. Mammy has the tea ready in a two quart can and she gives me some tea and a sandwich. I get it down me in a hurry and rush back down to the forge with tea and sandwiches for the others.

As soon as I get there, Daddy tells me to start pulling the bellows for Tom, as they have some coulters to weld before the shoeing begins. He tells Tom and Watt to have their tea and says he'll be back later. About an hour later, he arrives back from the the pub and smells of porter.

Welding coulters is tricky and involves lots of patience and skill. Watt tells me that Daddy once won first prize in a competition and was declared the best blacksmith in County Westmeath. Daddy knows all about welding and we're all very proud of that.

A coulter is a heavy piece of iron about half an inch thick, two feet long, and two or three inches wide. It cuts the sod in front of the soc of a plough, that in turn cuts the sod or scribe to a certain depth. The soc of the plough is attached to the mould board that turns the scribe upside down as the plough is pulled through the soil. The coulter fits in a slot and is held in place with an iron wedge. Mostly they wear down or get broken and pieces have to be welded onto them. The coulter and the piece to be welded are placed in the fire and heated to the point of burning.

Daddy, Tom, and Watt know when they're ready for welding by the little stars rising from the fire. About this time, they toss some borax into the fire. Borax is a clear powder like washing soda, and creates a blue flame when thrown on the fire. Watt tells me it works as a flux and cleaner, making the iron easier to weld. He learned all about being a blacksmith from Daddy.

Finally, the coulter is ready and Daddy grabs it with his gloved hand. He grabs the piece of iron with the pinchers. After taking them to the anvil, he places one on top of the other, and allows Tom to strike the first blow with the sledgehammer.

Daddy then drops the pinchers and starts hitting with the lump hammer. They keep on hitting until the coulter and piece of iron are all one and welded together. Meantime, sparks fly all over the place and I skidaddle over to the far side of the fire to save my feet. Meanwhile, I have to reach over and keep the bellows pulled, as it might take two more heats before the piece is finished and sharpened. Some sparks get on my arms and legs, but I just brush them off.

Later on, a big spark from the fire lands in my hair and I can't get rid of it. My hair starts to singe and then my scalp burns. Watt throws water on me from the little trough beside the fire. Daddy complains about that lousy coal he gets from Lovell's in Ballymahon. He tells Tom that there's good coal in Kildare if one could get it down to Moyvore.

Daddy's forge has two sections: one where we do the work, and the other known as the parlor forge. The parlor is an unroofed section where we keep scrap iron and spare parts. This section also houses the huge bellows, covered over with galvanized sheets. That's where I work on the bellows.

The bellows are supported on either side by two wooden posts. A round pipe sits on top of those posts and supports a pipe that goes through the wall over the fireplace. A short chain with a large ring attached to the end of this pipe is used to pull the bellows. Another round pipe through the wall at the hob level carries air to the fireplace. The bellows seem to take up a big section of the forge.

As I get tired from pumping the bellows, my eyes start to hurt from the heat and I slow down. Daddy gives the chain a jerk to wake me up. I can smell the drink on his breath. He tells me, "Remember what you're here for and don't fall asleep on the job."

They get the coulters welded just as the wheels are ready for shoeing. They start with the biggest wheels first. Tom and Watt grab the hoop, one on each side, with big iron pincers. They carry the hoop to the molded slab which has the shape and structure of a wheel, and lay it down around the wheel. Then Watt gets a round iron with a hook and levers down on the hoop with it. Tom goes around the wheel, hitting down the hoop with a hammer. Soon it's all down around the wheel and smoke and flame rise from the burning wood. Then Watt pours the cans of water on it to put out the flame. This allows him to lift the wheel into the water trough without getting burned. He gives it a few fast turns in the water to cool it off. Daddy gets on the other side, facing him, with two lump hammers. He hits the wheel and hoop to get them in the right position as Watt turns the wheel one spoke at a time. This takes five or ten minutes.

Meantime the water is getting low and I have to start hauling again. We get all twelve wheels shod, and then Daddy and Tom head for the pub and leave Watt and me to finish.

We have to make sure the fire is quenched, and we do this with the water from the trough. Clouds of ashes and smoke rise into the air. We get the place all swept up and start for home. Watt says it must be near seven o'clock because it seems nearly an hour since we stopped and said the six o'clock Angelus.

It was a great day and I enjoyed it, even though I'm wrecked tired. I'm really looking forward to the rabbit stew Mammy said she was cooking.

Burke's Forge, Moyvore

Serving Mass

It's my week to serve Mass. Four of us do it turn about, Fintan Murtagh, Pat Rowe, George Scally and myself. One of us serves Mass during the week, and on Sundays there are usually two of us.

I'm good at Latin and I can say it all off by heart, even if I don't understand it. My sister Margaret taught it to me.

The Moyvore church is as cold as our house. The church was built in the shape of a cross, with what we call the long aisle and the two short aisles, each with a gallery overhead. These galleries aren't used during the week, as only a few people attend Mass on weekdays. Joe Rodgers calls those people "the Moyvore Holy Mary's."

Father McManus and Father Daly have been transferred to another parish. Our new parish priest is Father Thomas O'Connell. He's a tall man who looks out over his glasses and makes a snorting sound up his nostrils. People say he's every bit as contrary as Father McManus. He never talks to us altar boys except to ask if we did this or that, or to send us to the priest's house for something he forgot.

The house is just twenty yards from the church. Mary Gallagher, the housekeeper, keeps wine for Mass in a pantry beside the kitchen that's nearly as big as our house. She gives me a little glass tray with water and wine and a small white linen cloth for Mass. I carry them to the vestry and get out the vestments for the day from the chest of drawers. The priest dresses from a table in the middle of the room. When I see him coming, I go to the altar and light the two candles on each side. During the week he says Mass quickly, with no sermon or collection, and it's usually over in half an hour. I don't like serving Mass during the week because I have to rush home and get ready for school. I only wanted to be an altar boy because Chris did it before me and I want to be as good as him. And besides, it makes Mammy happy.

After Holy Communion, I bring up the water and pour it over his fingers that are all brown from cigarettes. He rinses the Chalice by twirling it around in a circular motion. I like serving on Sundays, as it gives me a chance to show off in front of the other boys who don't serve.

Because this is my week to serve, I get to be lead server and do the collection in the main aisle, which has about eight or ten pews on each side, seating six people each. I start at the front and work toward the back, move up to the gallery, and then down the other side. I have to squeeze past a group of men sitting on the steps. All the pews in the gallery are full, except the one down at the front rail. Eddie Higgins always has that one to himself. He's a well-off farmer from Relic and always puts a two-shilling piece in the collection box—more than anyone else.

One Sunday, George Scally took up the collection and the two shillings was missing. Father Tom quizzed him about it and just about accused him of stealing. A week later, Eddie Higgins said he didn't put it in the box, as he had no change that day.

The sun is shining when we get out and nearly everyone has gone home. A football game is scheduled for Dalton's field today and I may go watch. The men moved the goal posts from Garahan's field last evening—they can't play there any more, because the owner has let the field out to meadow.

Up the way, Willie Rooney is starting home and I join up with him, but he keeps asking me embarrassing questions.

"How many beds do yis have in a room?"

"Two."

"How many rooms in the house?"

"Three."

"Well your mother and father take one room and that leaves two rooms for ten people. How many of you sleep in one bed?"

I tell him I'm going to look for mushrooms and I escape over the iron gate into Mearse's field.

The Chamber Pot

When I get home, the house is empty except for Daddy and Mammy, who are in bed with the flu.

Daddy calls out, "Is that you, Paidin? Come up here."

I go up to the room and he tells me to empty the poe. I look at the chamber pot, and it's overflowing with piss and shite. I'd like to tell him no, but I'm not that brave. I get it by the handles and it spills on my hands, and I'm dying with shame, and I hate him. When I get outside the cock crows and I say, "Shut your mouth or I'll throw it on top of you."

Daddy hears this, and I can hear him laughing. I get to the dung heap where we throw the ashes and empty it out. When I go back in he's still laughing, and asks me, "What did the cock say when he crew at you? Did he tell you not to spill it, Paidin?" He's laughing and so is Mammy. I hate them both.

I put it down, run to my room, and kneel by the bed, pulling the blanket over my head. I want to black out Willie Rooney, my father and mother, the piss-pot, my shame, and my anger and hate. I don't know how long I stay like that until Mammy comes and tells me to come down to the kitchen. She said not to mind that auld cock and gives me tea and bread.

Daddy shouts down, "Is he finished, Breenie?"

She says, "Yes, Joe."

"Come up here, Paidin."

I think, if he wants me to empty the pot again I'll just say no, even if he kills me. I go up and he says, "Never mind that auld cock, he's just a Protestant heathen." He gives me four pence and says, "Go to the shop and get yourself some sweets."

As I go out the door he's laughing again, but I don't care, because now I'm rich and I'll have lots of bull's eye sweets to take to the match. Later that evening they're all crowing at me and when I try to say something back, they tell me to shut up or, "I'll throw it on top of you."

A week later, it's Anne's turn. Mammy gives her Jeyes fluid and tells her to get the old scrubbing brush and scour the chamber pot. Anne is mad as hell, and I tell her she can crow all she wants now. We go out in Mearse's field and sit down with the poe between us upside down. She says, "You know, Paidin, this is the poe you were carrying when the cock crew at you. Let's pretend it's the head of someone we don't like."

We beat on it with stones and the white enamel starts to chip off till all the bottom is black. She says, "We'll get a beating for it anyway, so let us do a good job on it." We hit it some more, and even when we stop we can still hear the enamel cracking. Mammy calls Anne to know if she did that job she gave her. Anne goes in and puts the poe beside the bed. Not a word was said, and that damned poe never leaked.

The Pick

It's raining and the small chickens have the pick. Mrs. Keegan tells Mammy that if she gets a few horse hairs she'll show her how to take care of it. She says it's brought on by the rain and damp. They send me to the forge for horse hairs, and I peep in through the bellows hole in the wall to see if Daddy's there. I don't want to get caught and made to pull the bellows again. I don't mind doing it during school, but we're out for the summer holidays. Daddy isn't in the forge and I think he must be at the pub again, and Mammy won't be happy to hear that.

Mammy waited for him to come home all last evening. She sent us down to the pub several times to ask him to come home. I was afraid to go in the bar section and ask him. I went to the grocery end and told Mr. McQuaid, "Mammy wants Daddy to come home."

He said he would see to it that he came home right away, but he never did. Finally, Lilly Rodgers saw him lying in the ditch and helped him into the house. I was in bed, but not asleep. I heard Lilly say to Mammy, "Sure, Mrs. Burke, the poor auld divil is half frozen to death. I heard him as I was walking up from Mae's. He was afraid to come in and have to face yis again. You know, Missus Burke, it's not all his fault. McQuaid shouldn't be giving drink to people in that state. He helped Bernie Casey get on his horse five months ago and he fell off just up the road and split his skull and was killed stone dead."

I'm lying in bed listening to this, and I can see Bernie Casey's face. I saw and heard him screaming and kicking on the grass in front of Rooney's at the crossroads. They say he died on the way to the hospital. Mammy agrees with all Lilly said, and then thanks her.

When I go inside the forge, Watt is sharpening blades for a mowing machine; he won't need a fire for that. So, I decided to go in and ask him for horse hairs. "What do you think I am, a blasted barber or something? If there was a horse here I could get yis one, but there isn't. I tell you what; Mossy Dalton clipped the red chestnut mare yesterday, so if you go in to him he'll give you some."

I go back up the road to Daltons, who live just across the road from us. I don't like going there, because Mossy Dalton has just gotten home from the mental hospital. He was in for nine months this time. He claims he can always feel the madness coming on, but he can't do anything about it. They say he gets electric shocks in there. He said that was his fourth time and he'll never go in again.

Tom said it took six of them to hold Mossy down till the ambulance got there to take him. He said Mossy had the strength of at least ten men. All three of the Dalton men go off the head. I saw it happen once to their father, Morris. He's a big strong man who can jingle two fifty-pound weights behind his head. No one knows his real age, but he tells people he's seventy. Joe Rodgers says, "Isn't that a very handy age for getting the pension?" He claims he was born in Buenos Aires and all his papers, including his birth certificate, were burned in a fire. Bill Tormey says Morris isn't from around Moyvore any way or he would know it, as he himself is no Johnnie come lately to the place, like some people.

Johnny is the youngest Dalton and has been in the hospital many times. We can hear them at our house when they go off the head. Mrs. Dalton started riding a bike when she was seventy, and she rides all over the place, weaving from one side of the road to the other. She puts her hands in the middle of the handlebars, one on top of the other, like someone on a racing bike. Sometimes she says hello and sometimes she waits for you to speak and then she turns her head away. One time she stuck out her tongue at the priest. He said he didn't mind just so long as it wasn't wagging. Mammy says it's herself that should be taken in, instead of the sons.

Two large iron gates anchored to a shed on each side open into the Daltons' yard. The gates close over each other, with one held in place by a bolt to cement in the ground. I go in the one they always use and knock on the door. When Mrs. Dalton answers, she's wearing a man's hat on her head. I tell her Mammy sent me for a few horse hairs. She looks at me a in a strange sort of way and says, "What does she want horse hairs for?"

I tell her the chickens have the pick and Mrs. Keegan says she can cure them with a horse hair. I follow her to the horse shed, where she fills a sack with straw. She tells me "There should be horse hairs all through it, because Mossy himself clipped the mare there a few days ago. The straw will keep the chickens warm." She says, "Tell your mother I have some fresh buttermilk if she needs some."

I take home the bag of straw and tell Mammy about the buttermilk. She says, "Isn't that nice of her," and she sends me back for the buttermilk. This time Mrs. Dalton brings me into the scullery, where three brown crocks sit on a bench by the wall. She takes the board off the nearest one, and I see four dead mice floating in the buttermilk. She fills the can with a jug of buttermilk and drops one of the mice inside. She says, "Tell your mother the mouse will add flavor to it."

I want to tell her to keep it, but I'm scared one of the men might be going mad again and come and kill me. I take home the can of milk, and Mammy throws it out and says, "Isn't she the mad auld witch!"

Margaret brings in one of the little chicks and Mrs. Keegan puts a horsehair down its neck. She turns it back and forth between her thumb and forefinger. When she pulls it out, it's covered with little white worms. She does this several times and gets Mammy to do the next one. When she sees Mammy has the hang of it, she leaves. Out of ten chickens, only three of them die from the pick.

I like the little chicks when they're small and fuzzy, and not like the big hens that shite all over the place. When it rains, some of it gets trampled into the house and the only time the floor is dry is early in the morning. Before long it starts getting wet again. We have to scrub the floor on Fridays with a scrubbing brush, but first we scrape off the heavy stuff with a knife.

The Bees

Saturday evening is bath time, and Frank and Eddie get in the iron bath. I won't get in it anymore, because I'm too old. Mammy threatens to tell Daddy on me, but I know she won't because she doesn't like it when he beats us. I kneel down beside the bath and she washes my hair with red sunlight soap. She tries to comb it out and it hurts like hell and I wonder is she's combing or pulling it out by the roots. She complains I have a head like a hedgehog. When I try to complain she says, "Don't be a mollycoddle all your life."

Next day Frank and I go for the water, and then we're sent down to Mearse's field to get watercress for the dinner. Watercress is a green plant like spinach and grows close to water. We use it as a green vegetable when we have no cabbage. A little pond beside a stream down near the church has lots of watercress in it. After picking watercress, we decide to go to Mearse's, down past the church, and ask for apples. The housekeeper answers our knock and gives us two apples each. We swear to keep it a secret between ourselves, cause Daddy will kill us if he finds out.

One time Arthur Mearse came to our house and shouted in, "Are you up, Burke? It's nine-o clock and no one in the forge."

Daddy shouted, "I am, Mearse. Go down to that forge and wait there till I come down."

Arthur Mearse didn't show up again for over a week, and then he said, "By God, Joe, I'm your best customer and I get the least respect."

Daddy told him he works for money and not respect. And so the story was told by Mammy. The three Mearses have the biggest farms around Moyvore: Arthur Mearse, Bertie Mearse, and Bob Mearse.

Paheen O'Hearne said, "They're all right and not bad to work for, but what a pity it is they kick with the left foot."

I've never seen them play football and I ask Mammy if they did, and she says not to her knowledge. I told her what Paheen O'Hearne said and she explained, "It's some people's silly way of saying they're Protestant."

"But Joe is left-handed and he kicks with the left boot, and he's not a Protestant."

Teresa says, "Don't answer him, Mam, because that fellow will be asking questions till the cows come home."

The Mearses had another brother who committed suicide. Arthur said, "At least he did better than their brother Tom, who ran off with a woman from Ballymore and became a Catholic."

Between Mearse's house and the church, Frank and I walk past a field with a stone wall around it. The field is higher than the road, and a tree grows atop the wall. We notice a hole in the tree and bees flying around it. I tell Frank to get up on the wall and look to see if there's any honey inside the tree.

He says, "How can I do that without being stung?"

I give him a long stick and tell him to poke the hole with it and the bees will leave. I walk up the road a piece, and soon hear him shouting. I look back and he's running toward me with bees all around his head, both arms flailing. We run hell for leather for the church and slam the door behind us. A few of the bees get in, but they don't seem to bother us. I wonder if it's a sin to bring angry bees into God's house. But I know I've done worse, and this sin doesn't bother me too much. We wait a good while before venturing outside again. I don't know how long, but it's the longest we ever stayed in the church without being made to.

When we bring home the watercress, Mammy wants to know if we had to grow it. Frank made the mistake of telling Anne we went to Mearse's for apples and she told Daddy. He gave Frank and I the best beating we ever got. He took off his belt and used the buckle end on us. I got the worst of it. We were cowering down behind the door in the corner and Frank was a little behind me. Mammy tried to stop it by pleading with him, but she was afraid she'd get hit in the scuffle. When he stopped, there was blood behind my ear and a cut on my knee and my right thumb was swollen. Frank couldn't stop crying and Anne was crying. I think Daddy was maddest at me because I wouldn't cry.

When Tom heard about it, he said Daddy wouldn't have done it if he'd been there. I felt good about that, even though I knew he probably couldn't have done anything. Daddy often beat us when Tom was there. I never saw Daddy hit my mother, and neither did any of my brothers or sisters.

Chapter Five

Tom Gets Married

Tom has left the forge and gone to Ballymore to live with Nanny Molloy, a girl who was working in Ham's as a maid. Now this Nanny Molloy is one of the prettiest girls ever to come to Moyvore. Seán Rodgers says, "Sure you can't beat Tom Burke to pick a woman. She has long black hair and a pair of legs of which she shows plenty." Then he says, "She could pull my plough any day in the week."

Tom met Nanny at Hams where he had gone to shoe a horse. And from there on it must have been love at first sight because they got together every chance they got. The only things that seemed to separate them was work and sleep. Mammy was to remark later, "That poor Tom was doomed the minute that Molloy one clapped her eyes on him, his goose was cooked."

"Yes she had set her eye on him from the start, set the trap and Tom willingly sprung it."

Nanny hung around the forge every chance she got, till Daddy ran her off. He told Tom she was the talk of the village and would go with anything in britches. He told Tom to break it off with her because she was no good. Tom agreed and said he wouldn't see her anymore. That was all well and fine, until Mrs. Molloy came to our door demanding to see Tom. She seemed mad as hell and told Mammy her grandchild wasn't going to be known as Tom Burke's bastard. "Now you get that son of yours to stand up like a man and do what's right."

They did a lot of talking outside. Teresa grabbed me, pulled me into the house, and closed the door.

That night there's a lot of whispering going on in our house while us younger ones are in bed. I find out afterwards a collection was made to send Tom to England, but he never went. He went to live with Aunt Rose for three weeks and had a royal old time with the money. Then he went to Molloy's to live with Nanny.

Daddy, Joe, and Watt go to Molloy's with a rifle to bring Tom home, and they find him hiding under the bed. Daddy points the rifle at Tom and says, "Come out before I shoot you."

Tom tells him to go ahead and shoot because he isn't coming out. After a short stand off and some more threats, Daddy, Joe and Watt decide to leave. Before starting for home, Daddy tells Tom he is no longer a son of his and he is never to set foot in his house again. Next day the Gards (police) come to our house looking for the rifle. Mammy tells them she doesn't know anything about it. We all know it's up the chimney in the back room. That spells the end of Tom as a single man, and none of the Burkes are allowed to go to the wedding. Daddy tells us from now on we're never to speak to those Molloys at any cost. We found out later that the rifle didn't have any bullets in it, but Tom couldn't be too sure about that.

Teresa says she wishes Tom hadn't left, because she feels uneasy turning her head away from the Molloys when she meets them on the road. She says, "I don't see the difference between the Burkes and the Molloys anyway. They live in a council house and we live in a council house." She then asks Mammy, "Why did Tom have to leave?" Mammy tells her that is what happens sometimes when people fall in love.

"Is that what happened to you?" Margaret asks her. "Did you fall in love with Daddy?" She's standing behind Mammy, who is sitting by the fire darning a sock. Mammy has the sock pulled over an empty jam jar with the large hole in it facing upward. Margaret is pretending to comb Mammy's curly brown hair with her fingers.

"Now you better watch yourself, you little hussy. Be careful what you say talking to your mother like that, or I'll give you something to talk about."

"But Mam," Margaret says, "I only asked if you fell in love with him and did you run off with him?"

"That's none of your business! Now go out and get the turf for the fire."

"But Modleen, (Margaret, Teresa and Anne call her Modleen when they're teasing her, or when they want to get around her for something) why is it you never tell us about yourself when you were young?"

"What do you mean when I was young? I'm still young."

"I know you're still young, Modleen," Margaret says, "but tell me, did you feel you were on the shelf and had to get a man when you met Daddy?"

"Oh! but you're one bauld little faggot! On the shelf how do, and every man in Moyvore after me at the time."

She stops her darning and lays both her hands over the sock and jam jar. She has a little smile on her face as though she were thinking of something pleasant from her past

Then Margaret says, "If you weren't on the shelf, then why did you marry a man so much older than yourself? I mean he was thirty-four years old and you were only twenty-one. And you're about five feet seven inches tall and Daddy's hardly five feet eight, if he's that."

"What do you mean five feet eight? I'll have you know that your Daddy is five feet ten inches."

Margaret snorts, "Five feet ten how do. I think, Modleen, you must not have been wearing your glasses that night when you met him."

Margaret winks at Teresa, "I mean it was at night when you met him, right, Modleen?"

Mammy pauses in thought for awhile, as though reliving that part of her past. Then she says, "Not that it's any of your business, but we fell in love, if you must know."

"And if anything happened to Daddy, would you get married again, Modleen?"

"No, I suppose not, he's the only one, unfortunately."

"And tell me this, Modleen," asks Margaret, "before you got married, how would yis meet? Would you go across to him in Digby's old house, or would he sneak in the window at Grennan's to see you?"

Mammy takes off her glasses and starts to wipe them with her soiled handkerchief. Then she says, "My, but you are one right little fairy. We didn't do things like that in those days, not like the young ones of today, with their 'Here I am and into bed, and goodbye.'"

Margaret laughs, "But our little Modleen wouldn't do that, would you, Modleen?" Serious again Margaret asks, "Well tell me then, Modleen, why did Tom do it? I mean why did he run off with that Nanny Molloy one?"

The change of topic seems to come as a surprise to Mammy and the expression on her face changes from a little grin to a frown.

That ends it. Mammy would never have anyone say anything about Tom. He was always the woolly lamb of the family (favorite). Every Friday evening since he was sixteen she would have his shirt and collar and tie ironed for him. She'd help him with his tie and brush the hairs from his shoulders to make sure he looked the part going out. Watt said she never did anything like that for him. Mammy pushes Margaret away from her and continues with her darning.

Years later when I thought about the close relationship between Tom and Mammy, I wondered was it because she had three girls first and was happy when she finally gave birth to a baby boy. Or was Tom a buffer between her and Daddy? Maybe it was a bit of both and more.

When Aunt Rose paid us a visit once, Frank heard her say to Teresa, "Your mother never cut the umbrella cord when Tom was born."

Now the only umbrellas I ever saw didn't have cords on them. So I ask Teresa about it. She laughs and says, "You silly little bugger, it's the umbilical cord."

I ask her, "What is an umbilical cord?"

She asks, "Have you ever seen a calf being born?"

"Yes, I saw one at Rooney's," I say.

"Well then, you know the part that looks like a gut that goes from the calf to the cow. That's the umbilical cord."

And then she says she doesn't want to talk about it anymore.

I'm sorry for asking, because I can't see what that has to do with anything.

Carrying Water

Anne and I have to go for water to the pump in Moyvore. It's a green pump with cement walls round it. Mammy says, "That pump wouldn't be there but for your Daddy. He was the one who kept on to the county council to get it. Some of the people wouldn't sign the petition for it, and said the only reason Joe Burke wanted a pump was so he could shoe the cartwheels at his forge across the road."

Mammy says there are some bad and begrudging articles in the world, and what goes around comes around. Now they're all only too glad to use the pump, even the farmers when their wells run dry.

We carry the water in galvanized buckets. We put the buckets on a brush handle and carry them between us. Sometimes they slide all the way over to my side because I'm shorter than Anne, and then we have to stop to fix them.

They're tarring the road from the Baltackin crossroads to Moyvore, using a black tar boiler for boiling the tar with a spout at the back to fill the tar buckets. One man pours tar on the road, another spreads it with a yard brush, while another shovels stones on it from a pony and cart. Finally a big steamroller goes over it to even out the road.

I ask Anne, "Wouldn't it be great if we had a clean tar boiler for water at home? That way all we'd have to do is fill the water from the spout."

She says, "Don't be so stupid; you can't use a tar boiler for water."

Sometimes we have to go to the pump twice, because Mammy uses the water for washing clothes when the barrels are dry. I'll be glad when the road wears down—then the stones won't hurt my feet as much. I got a stone bruise four days ago and it got all soft and puffy. I stuck a pin in it this morning and let the stuff out of it. It gets better faster that way, but now I have to walk on the side of my foot. Sometimes I stub my toe on the road and it pulls the skin down from under my toenails, and that takes even longer to heal.

67

When I go down the fields to gather sticks for the fire, the wet grass and thistles catch in my foot and it gets real sore. Anne has shoes and doesn't have to go in her bare feet like the boys. Once Daddy was about to hit Teresa for something she was supposed to do and didn't, but Mammy stopped him saying, "No, Joe, no! not the girls." Teresa was lucky, she only got a few slaps on the arse. I hate him when he beats us, but I do wonder why is it all right to beat the boys?

We get the water home and Anne is singing some song she heard on Shaw's wireless. Margaret tells her if she ever gets any money for singing to give it back. Anne tells her, "I can sing better than you, you redheaded bitch." Mammy gives her a scelp of the dishcloth across the face and she runs to her room crying. That's the end of her song for the day.

Mrs. O'Kelly's Bike

"George Scally. Can you tell me what is the Trinity?" George stands up, but he doesn't know the answer. We all stand up when Mrs. O'Kelly asks us a question.

"Did you do your home work last night?"

"No, ma'am."

"And why not, may I be so bold to ask?"

"Because I forgot, ma'am."

"You forgot. You were so busy. Is that it?"

"No, ma'am."

"Get up here!"

She gives George two slaps across his hands with the stick.

"Paidin Burke!" She never calls me Pat or Patrick, because her son is called Patrick. She calls me the Irish Paidin, and the way she says it makes my name sound like Paw-deen. I hate it. I wish I'd been called Mike or Bill or Phillip—anything other than Paidin.

"Can you tell me what is the Trinity?"

I stand up and answer, "Three divine persons in one God, ma'am."

"Did you do your home work?"

"Yes, ma'am." I wonder why she has to ask me when she has my jotter right there on her desk in front of her.

"What was your homework?"

"A composition on the life of St. Patrick, ma'am."

She picks up my jotter and it has a good few ink splotches on it. She says, "Where did you write it, in a pigsty?"

"No, ma'am." She reads it and asks, "What did St. Patrick use to describe the Trinity?"

"The shamrock, ma'am."

"All right, you may sit down."

The two classrooms are the same size; one for the smaller children and one for the bigger children. The teachers sit near the fireplace in the corner of each room. Their legs get all red from the fire and there are red spots on them called brackets. Every family with children going to school is expected to give one horse load of turf each year for the fire, but there's never enough, and to spare it we gather sticks.

There are twelve desks in each room, and each desk seats two children. They're made of cast iron, and the seat backs and tops are wood. The top has spaces for our books and two inkwells. There's a large space between the front desks and the wall separating the two rooms. This space is used for reading and history class. We also call it the place of divine punishment, because that's where she calls us up to get slapped.

Mrs. O'Kelly calls out, "Paidin Burke, you go for the water." We get a fresh bucket of water each day for their tea.

I say, "Yes, ma'am," and I try going around the back wall so as not to attract her attention. But she calls me up front to the big space and looks at my feet.

"Your shoes are not very good, are they?"

"No, ma'am." I'm wearing old shoes that came down from Chris. There are two big holes in the soles and this morning I made insoles from newspaper for them. The paper didn't last long, because there was snow on the ground and it got all wet and was coming out in pieces. Before going in to school I took out all the paper.

George Scally has new boots he got for free from the government. The priest went to their house and asked his mother why George hadn't been to school for two weeks. She said it was because he had no shoes. He told her Jesus had no shoes. She said, "I know that, Father. But if he were on the earth today, he would be driving a big new car like you. He wouldn't be going to school in his bare feet." She closed the door in his face.

The Burkes cannot get free boots because Daddy is a tradesman. I wish he wasn't.

"Hold up your feet," Mrs. O'Kelly tells me.

I hold them up one at a time. The soles of my feet are showing and they're reddish purple. I hear a few snickers from the class. I lower my head and my face is redder than my soles. I wonder why she sends me to get the water when there are older boys in the class room. Then I think it must be that the older ones are preparing for their confirmation. I ask Teresa about it and she say's that might be the reason, or it could be because she hates the Burkes.

Mrs. O'Kelly looks at me for a spell and says, "All right you may go and get the water."

I go out to the cloakroom and get the bucket. There's some water in it that will serve to prime the pump. Flakes of snow are falling, but I don't feel the cold because I'm hot all over from the embarrassment. I bite my lip and a small bit of blood comes away on the back of my hand. I swear I'll get even with that white-haired auld bitch for showing me up before the whole class.

After filling the bucket at the pump, I go across the road to Daddy's forge. I take a new horse nail from the shoeing box and when I get back to school I flatten both of her bicycle tires with the nail. I know she'll have no doubt that I did it, but she'll never prove it. From this time on I will do anything and everything I can to her, or my name isn't Pat Burke.

70

Back From Doon

Seán is back from Doon, County Limerick. He says he was doing all the work on the farm and in the shop for no pay. Meanwhile, the owner was drinking a lot. He only had his fare as far as Mullingar. Mammy says that he hasn't much to show for a year and a half of service.

Chris, Frank, and I are at the crossroads flogging a top when we see him walking down the road. I think he looks bigger and taller, and he can sleep with Watt now that Joe isn't home any more. He stays with us flogging the top 'til near dark.

A top is a piece of wood about three inches long and two inches across. We make them from ash suckers. One end is shaped oval like an egg, with an iron stud driven in the end. We spin the top on the road and whip it to keep it going. The whip is a leather bootlace called a fong, tied to a piece of a stick about two and a half feet long. By whipping the top with the spin we can keep it going up and down the road.

We draw two chalk lines on the road about three feet apart. Before anyone can play they must run about twenty yards and jump to the first line, then hop on one foot to the second line. Meanwhile they must chant "I can run and I can hop. I can spin and flog my top." The one flogging can ask anyone to join in. Two can play at a time. We don't ask Seán to do the run and hop because he's too big and we're just happy to see him. And I think he's happy to see us.

Ferreting

Watt asks me if I want to go ferreting with him. Mammy says, "How can he go ferreting after he's been in bed two days with the flu? And besides, what will happen if someone sees him and tells Mrs. O'Kelly? Then we'll have the priest up to us and he'll say 'Paidin can't go to school, but he can go traipsing all over the fields.'"

Watt says, "Just send that priest to me and I'll tell him a thing or two. And besides, no one will see us."

"Oh, sure you'll tell him! Watt Burke the big hero. Well, let me tell you, Watt Burke, if you keep messing with those holy priests they will put a curse on you like was put on Desi Mahon."

"Oh, Mam, you know well Desi Mahon died from natural causes."

" Maybe so, but as I heard it someone was laughing during Mass and Father McManus said we would all know who it was before the year is out—and just look what happened."

Watt doesn't like Father Tom since he accused Chris of drinking Guinness on the day of the all Ireland football final. As it turned out, it was a new drink in Moyvore called Coca Cola and it looks like Guinness when poured into a glass. Watt said it was the Hams that told him, because Father Tom always has his arse stuck in their house, and they're big farmers, and he has no time for the poor people.

Watt went down to Father Tom and asked who told him Chris was drinking Guinness. When Father wouldn't tell him, Watt asked him to take off his priest's collar or turn it backwards and he'd beat it out of him. Father Tom called him a blackguard and slammed the door in his face.

Anyway, Watt tells Mammy, "We're only going up as far as Halston. I just want to take a look at that hill. They say it's walking alive with rabbits. Jody Carey paid twenty pounds just for the trapping of it last year."

"And pray tell how do you intend to go there without been seen?"

"We can cut across Dalton's field to the Baltackin crossroads and take the Dalystown Road from there. Sure there's never anyone on that road."

"Doesn't your brother Tom live right under that hill and can't he tell you about it?"

"My brother Tom doesn't know his arse from his elbow. If a rabbit jumped up in front of him, he'd think it was a cat."

"You should go and wash out you mouth with Jeyes Fluid before you go anywhere."

I can just see Watt with Jeyes fluid in his mouth.

I'm thrilled to be off ferreting with Watt. He has a little yellow ferret with a long tail and red eyes. He bought the ferret from someone in Ballymore for two pounds and says it can see in the dark with the red eyes. He carries the ferret in a wooden box, or sometimes just slips him inside the pocket of his black topcoat.

We have a black and white dog called Spot we got from Tom Monaghan and he chases a hare in Mearse's nine-acre field behind our house nearly every day. Watt says the hare is only playing with him, and if the hare only had two legs, Spot still wouldn't catch him. The hare is usually two fields away and Spot is still barking.

We're crossing Dalton's field when Spot raises a hare, and off he goes. He won't come back no matter how Watt whistles for him. He says he'll drown that dog one of these days and get a good dog.

We get to Tom's house and he tells us not to dare go up that hill with a dog as there are "no trespassing" signs up all over the place, and we'll get a summons for sure. He asks Watt if he heard about the stray dogs killing Ham's sheep two days ago. Watt says he didn't.

"Well, they killed a sheep, and now the lands are posted with signs saying these lands are poisoned."

Watt says, "That being the case, we'd better start locking up that auld dog of ours at night. That or get rid of him. If he's one of those dogs that get poisoned, that would be proof and we'd be held liable for any and all sheep killed."

Tom agrees with Watt saying, "It might be a good idea. And it's better to be sure than sorry."

"Have you got a fag?" Watt asks.

Tom says, "I can let you have one."

"Well, one is better than none. Has Mrs. Reynolds at the shop got any over there?"

"She might have, but sure she won't give them to you. She barely knows you, and you're not a regular customer."

Watt says it won't hurt to chat her up anyway. Even though the war is long over, most things are still rationed. We need coupons to get most things including butter, tea, sugar, flour, all the way down to razor blades.

Daddy gets upset talking about rations because it's only been a hundred years since two million Irish people died of starvation while the English were shipping food out of the country to feed their troops overseas. Now the Irish government allows the food to be sent to England to help feed their starving people because of their war with Germany. Daddy says, "You can always trust the government to get it wrong."

Watt usually gets seventy fags a week from John McQuaid. He calls it his allowance for the week, but the trouble is they only last him four or five days, and then he has to go begging for more. One time I went for his fags and McQuaid only gave me fifty. Watt then went down to McQuaid and they had a big fight over it.

Mrs. Reynolds has a small little shop a few hundred yards up the road from Tom's house. People say she has everything from a shovel to a gramophone needle. She tells Watt over the half door that she hasn't got a single cigarette in the place.

"God, missus," he says, "just sell me ten players and I'll say a Rosary for you."

"Watt, I don't care if you say ten Rosaries. I can't sell you any for the simple reason that I don't have any."

We go down the road to the end of her garden and Watt sees a burrow. He puts the ferret in and we get out two rabbits. We go back to Mrs. Reynolds again. Now she tells Watt, "I'll give you ten players for a rabbit."

He says, "No way. I'll give you the two for thirty players. And look, one of them is still alive, so you can keep him till you're good and ready to put him in the pot."

"God," she says, "Watt Burke, you're an awful tinker. Okay, I'll give you twenty players and no more."

Back down in the fields again, Watt sits on a stonewall smoking one of those fags till it burns his fingers. I can't understand it, but he looks like he enjoys them mightily.

When we get home, we learn that Spot hasn't come back. The next morning, I find him near the school with his head down and froth coming from his mouth. Joe Rodgers says, "That dog looks like he got poisoned." He tells me to me to lock him up and don't give him any food or water for three days. I do this and he gets sick all over the shed, but he lives.

The next day one of the priest's two Irish setters is found dead.

Collecting Bills

"Breenie, would you ever get down that ledger till I see what we've got?" says Daddy.

Mammy takes the ledger from behind one of the willow pattern dishes on the dresser and starts to read. "One set of shoes, twelve and six pence. Two removals and hoof repair, three and six pence. Repair one spring tooth harrow, eleven shillings. Weld one coulter, six shillings. Make two linchpins, two shillings."

"How much does that come to, Breenie?"

"One pound eight shillings."

"Alright, will you make out a bill for that and send it up to him?"

"Okay! And what about that bill for Pat Donohue?"

"Yes, that one too, and Tom Murtagh owes a bill, but just take care of those two first and we'll go from there."

Mammy makes out the two bills and hands them to Anne. "Take the one up to Somers first, and then you can go to Donohue's."

I know well by the look on Anne's face that she wants to say, "No, I won't go." But Daddy is there and she knows better. Mammy says, "Take Paidin with you in case you get lost." I wonder how can she get lost and she going on twelve years old, and that's over a year and a half older than me. I don't want to go, but I know I have no choice seeing as Daddy's home. I could say no, but I'd get a beating and he'd still make me go. And even if I don't have to go, he'd find some reason to beat me anyway. So I have no choice but to hit the road with Anne.

When Anne and I get to Baltackin crossroads, I point out Scally's little field where George and I had the feed of wild garlic a few weeks ago. A short distance further on is Scally's house, and in the field across the road is the well where George and I sucked the goats. We didn't really suck them, but we told all the children at school we did.

What we did was lay on our backs with our heads under the udder and squirt the milk in our mouths. We did this turn about while one of us held the goat. My face was all kinda sticky, and I had flies all around me on the way home. Mammy said I smelled like a dirty dog. She gave me a bar of red sunlight soap and a basin and sent me out to the barrel of rain water to wash myself, saying I wasn't to come back till I smelled half human. She couldn't believe anyone would eat garlic and drink goat's milk at the same time. She told Daddy about it later and I think it was the last time I ever heard him laugh.

As we turn on to the Dalystown Road there's a council sign and I read it out loud to Anne, "Dancer road under repper."

Anne takes a fit of laughing and says, "Danger road under repair, you clown. God, but you get more stupid by the day."

I tell her to shut her big mouth or she'll be going the rest of the way on her own. I know she has no sweets so I don't care. I'd go back home in a minute. She says to me, "Alright, I won't tell anyone when we get home."

Of course it was the first thing she told them all when we got back.

Peter Ahearn's is the first house on the Dalystown Road. He's a cobbler and has a short leg. One of his boots has a sole nearly four inches thick. He put two uppers on my boots a few months ago. We continue on till we get to Somer's house and Anne hands the folded bill to a woman at the door. She reads it and says, "Let me see what I can do." She returns after awhile and hands a white envelope to Anne, who says thanks, and we leave.

Down the road a little piece, Anne feels the envelope and says, "You know, Paidin, there's money in that, I can feel the coins. Do you know how seldom people ever give us money? We must have gone to eight different places in the last few months and this is the first time we got any money. It's always, 'Tell your father I'll see him next week,' or 'My husband is off selling cattle soon and he'll settle up with him.'" She asks me, "Do you think Mammy or Daddy would miss a sixpence if we took it?"

I say, "Yes, they certainly would, and if you take it, I'll tell them."
She sighs, "I suppose you're right."

We get back to the Baltackin crossroads and take the Robinstown Road on the way to Mearsecourt. There are no houses on the Robinstown Road; it's just used as a short cut from the Mullingar Road to Mearsecourt. Most all the land on either side of the road is owned by Arthur Mearse. He was willing to sell the council a full acre of land here for our house, but Daddy said that was too far from the forge. Mammy said instead we wound up with half an acre nearer the forge and the pub.

Pat Donohue is a small farmer who comes to Moyvore every six weeks or so to have his horse shod. He only brings the horse and cart when he has a piece of machinery to get fixed. Otherwise he rides a bike, leading the horse. He used to ride the horse till it shied one time and threw him, and that was the last time he rode a horse. One time, Chris had to ride the horse home for him, as he had a few drinks too many. Pat usually goes in to Moyvore about eleven o'clock and stays till late evening. Sometimes on his way home he stops into our house with eggs and rashers and Mammy cooks them for him.

"Are you hungry, Pat?" she once asked him.

"Did you say hungry, Mrs. Burke? I could eat a scabby baby through the rails of a chair."

The last time Pat came to the forge I got caught for pulling the bellows. Watt was left to shoe the horse while Pat and Daddy went to the pub. On their return, Daddy put an iron in the fire to heat. Then he took down from the wall the two foot piece of a shovel handle with a piece of rope through the end. This is called a grin. He slipped the rope over the horse's upper lip and twisted the handle till the horse's lip stood out like a handball. He had Watt hold this handle while Pat Donohue held the horse's mouth open. Then he brought the red-hot iron from the fire, and holding the horse's tongue down over his lower teeth he inserted the hot iron. I stood dumfounded as I heard the flesh sizzle, and I thought it was cruel. Next he got a hand full of salt and rubbed it in the horse's mouth. Watt told me later that it was to cure the lampers that were like lumps or blisters at the back of the tongue or throat. He said if they weren't taken care of they would keep growing and the horse wouldn't be able to eat or breathe.

"There now, Pat," Daddy said, "you're all set. He may be a bit slow to eat for a few days, but he'll be alright." As well as training as a blacksmith, Daddy had some early training as a veterinarian and often called on that experience to help the local farmers.

When Anne and I get to Donohue's place, she hands in the piece of paper. We hear talking inside the house and a man's voice saying, "Sure I took care of that already, but let me handle it."

Pat Donohue comes out with a sack in his hand and goes to a shed that has turkeys in it. He puts a turkey in the sack with it's head sticking out a hole in the side and hands it to Anne. He tells her, "This is a young turkey getting ready to lay. Give it to your father and tell him I said it's part of the deal we made. He'll know what it's all about."

Anne tells him thank you and we head for home with our turkey.

I think to myself, won't Mammy be surprised when we land in with a turkey. Anne is so happy she could skip without a rope. She says, "You know, Paidin, this is the very first time we got something everywhere we went. Mammy won't believe it. Then again it just might be the worst thing that ever happened to the two of us. Because now, we'll be expected to do this all the time, and Mammy will make the excuse that the two of us are lucky."

I can't wait for Frank and Eddie to grow up so they can do it. Anne says to me, "Maybe we should let the turkey go and say nothing about it."

I tell her, "Don't be stupid! We can't do that, because Pat Donohue will ask Daddy about it the next time he goes to the forge. Even if we did let it loose, it wouldn't last one night because those fields are full of foxes. Sure, I saw two when I was picking the potatoes for Ned Flanagan."

Vexed now, Anne says, "Maybe you are right, but if you say stupid to me again it will be the last breath you'll ever draw till the day you die."

I mutter, "Alright. I won't say it, even if you are."

On the Chapel Road between the Robinstown Road and our house the ditches are loaded with red haws. We've walked about four miles and the hunger is getting the better of us. We only had one slice of bread when we got home from school. We put the turkey down and start eating the haws. We stay at it till our tongues are sore from chewing on the stones, and by the time we get home the two of us have pains in our bellies. Anne lays the sack in the middle of the floor with the turkey's head sticking out.

Mammy looks at it and says, "Glory, honor and praises to God and his Holy Mother what do yis have there?"

Anne says, "It's a turkey."

"Sure, I'm not blind, I can see it's a turkey, but where did yis get it?"

Anne tells her, "We got it from Pat Donohue and he said that Daddy knows all about it."

"Well, I declare to God what men won't get up to in a pub is no one's business. We often took chickens for payment in the old days, but this is the fist time we ever got a turkey. Now, what are we to do with it? It's a good while till Christmas to have to be feeding it."

Anne tells her it's not for Christmas, "It's a laying turkey and maybe if it lays a whole lot of eggs and hatches them we can have a whole lot of turkeys just like the Rooneys."

Mammy says, "That's right, and if you live horse, you'll get grass. Anyway, put it out in the shed with the hens for now, and tomorrow we'll figure out what to do with it."

Thinking about the four hens and the cock, I think, isn't that turkey bigger and stronger than that cock, and won't he beat the shite out of him? Now we'll see who's king of the roost around here. I'm so pleased with the thought of it that I volunteer to take the turkey to the hen house. When I put it inside the door, the cock and the hens go wild, cackling and flying all over the shed. They have never seen a turkey before and they aren't happy about sharing their coop with one.

Back in the house again, Anne has given the envelope to Mammy, who seems pleased. The pot of potatoes is ready for teaming. Teresa takes it outside and with the help of two old dishcloths, she teams the water out of them. She slips the metal lid back enough so the potatoes won't fall out and tips the pot over on its side. In cold weather we use that metal lid as a hot water bottle—we put it on the fire till it's good and hot, then wrap it in a cloth and put it in bed with us. Daddy and Mammy have a real hot water bottle. We have only one lid for the pot and the oven and sometimes Mammy needs it to bake a cake. When the cake is in the oven she puts the lid on it and puts hot coals on the lid.

As the water runs off, Teresa tips it more until it's upside down and all the water is gone. She brings it back in and empties the potatoes out on the table. At this point, whoever can stand the heat the best gets the best potatoes. Mammy puts chopped carrots and parsnips on our plates and white sauce. She sits at the fire having hers. She has the plate in her lap and a half-pound of butter on the floor beside her. We have fresh buttermilk Chris brought home from Brennan's last evening.

Watt sits at the end of the table and he has a fried egg with his carrots and parsnips. Teresa is at the other end, near the door. Chris takes the other chair and Anne, Frank, and Edmund and I stand wherever we can. The stool is out in the shed waiting to be fixed. Frank's sauce is all gone and he asks Chris if he can dip his spud in his. Chris tells him, "You can dip it, but don't roll it."

Mammy puts some potatoes beside the fire for Daddy, who hasn't come home yet. Pretty soon there's nothing left but a pile of skins on the table. They'll be mixed with meal for the hens tomorrow. I'm looking forward to tomorrow—hoping to see a big turkey and cock fight.

Chapter Six

No Lunch

Lunchtime starts each day after we say the Angelus. The teacher says, "Class dismissed!" and we all scatter in different directions. Most children bring their lunch in brown paper bags or wrapped in a newspaper. Those who live near the school are allowed to go home for lunch, including the Tormeys of the village and us.

An iron gate across from the school leads to Mearse's nine-acre field. We use it as a short cut to our house so we don't have to go around by the crossroads, which takes longer. We're glad that we can go home, because some of the time we don't have any lunch, and if we stayed at school we'd just have to watch the other children eating.

Most times Mammy has a pot of potatoes on to boil, but sometimes we can't wait for them, as we only get a half hour for lunch. She takes some out with the tongs and puts them on the table. We try to cut them, sometimes they're still hard. We take one each in a piece of paper to eat on the way back.

We juggle the potatoes from hand to hand, cooling them down. Sometimes we have stirabout left over from the morning. If we have buttermilk to go with it, that makes it all the better. Today we run home only to see the pot of potatoes sitting in the middle of the floor and Mammy sitting by the fire talking with Mrs. Crinegan. My belly hurts and I'm close to tears. Anne is crying. We had no breakfast this morning and now it looks as if we will have to go without lunch. I say to Anne, "I'm so hungry, my belly thinks my throat has been cut."

Teresa asks Mammy, "Why didn't you put on the spuds?"

Mammy looks surprised to see us and says, "I didn't realize it was so late in the day."

Teresa says, "You mean you were too busy talking."

Mrs. Crinegan tells Teresa she's a bauld brat talking to her mother like that. Mammy tells us she will bake a big cake this evening when we get the buttermilk from Peggy Mahon. Anne asks her if she will she make a nice black bread like the one Murtaghs have.

I know well that Anne and I will have to go for the buttermilk, but we don't mind that because Peggy Mahon is nice and she'll give us tea, bread and jam. It's over a mile to Mahon's on a gravel road with no houses. The road is all right in daylight, but at night it's really scary, mostly because of Mrs. Crinegan's ghost stories. If a rabbit moves in a ditch or a bird flutters or we hear a noise, then we think it's a ghost for sure. Peggy Mahon usually keeps us talking for ages, even though she has the buttermilk just sitting there. Mammy says the poor crather (creature) gets lonely there on her own. Sometimes she puts a big lump of homemade butter in the can of buttermilk and we're delighted. When this happens, we know we'll have butter and bread in the morning and butter for our spuds in the evening.

By the time we get back from lunch that day, the children are going in to school. The teachers have a bell to ring, but they seldom use it. Mrs O'Kelly hits the window with her knitting needle to call the children. When the priest asks her how the glass got broke she said some of the boys threw a stone at it.

That afternoon, I get two slaps for throwing wet blotting paper at Kathleen Early. Liam Mahon gets two for having too many sums wrong. And George Scally gets two for talking. George is muttering under his breath, and she calls him up to give him more.

He says, "If you hit me again, I will tell you something about your daughter Carmel that won't like to hear."

"What did you say?" she demands. Her face is as white as her hair and she's shaking.

Before he can respond, she shouts, "Get out of my school."

As he goes through the door, she says, "Don't come back without a written apology."

Everyone knows her daughter Carmel just had a baby out of wedlock in Drogheda. Even I feel George was wrong to say such a thing. That is a matter for the grown ups.

Upset by the whole thing, Mrs. O'Kelly lets school out an hour early. Later on, Mammy says it was good enough for her. But then she says, "Ah, sure maybe he shouldn't have said it though."

I'm delighted because we can go for the buttermilk early and I look forward to the tea and bread and jam.

Cleaning Drains

Watt has left the forge to go cleaning drains with Jody Carey. He said he couldn't get along with Daddy anymore. "And furthermore," he says, "neither could the good Lord himself get along with him. And what was the use of me slaving away in the forge while he was drinking it away in the pub?"

Mammy says, "More's the pity, because he says you have the makings of a better tradesman than your brother Tom, and weren't you learning a trade?"

Watt says he knows enough about the trade. "Anyway, I know just as much as any blacksmith and if I don't then maybe he's not a good teacher. Maybe if he had stayed out of the forge, I could have made a good business out of it. Well it doesn't matter now, and besides I made more money in the last month than I would for two months in the forge."

Mammy says, "If you made so much money, how come you don't have enough for cigarettes?"

"Now, Mam, if I told you once I told you a thousand times, I won't get paid till the job is done. I wonder if McQuaid would let me have enough till then?"

Mammy says, "I doubt it. We already owe a huge bill there."

He tells Anne to ask McQuaid for: "Sixty players, three twenty packs, and tell him I'll pay him Friday when I get paid."

Mrs. Mc Quad is tending the shop when Anne and I walk in. Anne asks her for two pan loaves, one pound of butter, two pounds of sugar, a quarter pound of tea, a half stone of flour, a half stone of brown flour, and a quarter stone of cracked oats, Bendigo tobacco, and a packet of Max Smile razor blades.

After putting them on the counter, Mrs. McQuaid says, "I do hope you have the money to pay for this."

Anne says, "Mammy said to put it on the book."

Mrs. McQuaid takes the black ledger book from behind the cash register and says, "There's already a bill for six pounds and four shillings, and I told you last time no more credit until it's settled. Now I'll let you have it this time, but tell your mother this is the last."

Anne says, "Watt wants sixty players and he said he will pay you when he gets paid."

Mrs. McQuaid sniffs and says, "You don't say. So Watt Burke wants credit too, does he? Well I suppose I can trust him once, but you tell him the minute he gets paid to come in here and settle."

My face is burning with embarrassment and I glance at the two other people in the shop to see if they're listening. Only a thin wall separates the grocery from the bar, and I know everyone in the bar can hear us. Mrs. McQuaid packs the shopping in brown paper bags and Anne puts two pence on the counter and asks for two pence worth of sweets.

"You don't say! Two pence worth of sweets. Now you know we don't sell sweets by the penny, we sell them by the quarter pound, half pound, or pound, not by the penny." She puts her hand in the jar and takes out what she can hold between her fingers and puts them on the counter. Anne grabs the candy and we rush out the door.

Outside she says, " I hate that auld bitch, and that's the last time I'm ever going to that shop without money, even if Mammy kills me. And why do you and me have to go everywhere while everyone else sits on their arse? Why can't we be like all the other people and pay for things when we get them, and not be getting embarrassed in front of people?"

"Because we don't have any money," I say.

She says, "Paidin, you know you are pure stupid. And there's another thing, how come we always have more boils and sores on us than other children?"

I think about that and touch the boil on the back of my neck. It's almost better, since I bruised the stuff out of it yesterday. The worst one I ever had was on my belly a month ago. George Scally and I had one of our usual fights and he hit me with a stick right on the boil. It was the worst pain I ever felt and the first time I cried in a long time— also one the few times he ever got the better of me.

"What are you talking about? You don't have any boils," I tell her.

"I know, and that's why I don't like being near you or Frank, because yis are always full of them. And now the two of yis have ringworm. Now tell me, Paidin, how do you do it, I mean how come you always get everything?"

I think to myself: How do I know? How do I know why I have scabs in my head and scaly white stuff falls out when I scratch it? How do I know why my nose is always running? How do I know why there are always scabs on my legs? And why do you always ask such stupid questions? I know that I can't ask you why because if I do, you won't give me any sweets, but when I get them off you, then I'll speak up. Instead I say, "I don't know. Maybe it's because we're not smart like you."

She says, "You don't have to tell me what I already know."

I look at the ringworm sores on my arms, and they've almost disappeared. They started as little red spots and grew till they were nearly as big as the top of a cup. Mammy said we must've been in contact with some cows or calves, because that's where ringworm comes from. At first they were just itchy, and then they got raw and sore. Doctor Joyce gave us ointment and we put it on them for a week, but it did no good.

Seán Rodgers told us, "You might as well piss on it as put that ointment on." He said he had it a year earlier and finally had to go to the seventh son of a seventh son healer down in County Cavan, who cured it for him. He says, "Doctor Joyce isn't worth a damn, there

85

must be up to ten different diseases in the world and he gives the same red bottle for all of them." Seán told Mammy that Dan Garahan nearly died in the Mullingar Hospital with the shingles after going to Dr. Joyce for six weeks. When he couldn't cure Dan, he sent him to the hospital. Seán said, "Them shingles are dangerous, kind of like ring worm that starts around your belly, and if they go all the way around they strangle you and you die. Oh they say it was touch and go with him, as to whether he would live or die."

I know I wouldn't be inclined to trust that doctor too much. I wonder if the ringworm had gone around my arms would I have died. Then I think how could I die when it wasn't on my belly? But then maybe I could have lost an arm—and what then? I wouldn't be able to carry water or fight George Scally.

Daddy chewed some of his tobacco and spit it on our ringworm and Mammy put bandages on them she'd ripped from an old sheet. He did this for three days and our ringworm was nearly better in a week.

As we continue toward home, Anne peers into the sack. "That mean auld rip, she only gave me eight bulls eyes for two pence. I'll give you two, and one to Frank, and one to Eddie." She hands me the two bull's eyes.

Immediately I say, "Thanks, stupid!"

"That's the last time I'll ever give you anything," she swears.

Watt is waiting for us at the crossroads. "Did yis get the cigarettes?"

Anne says, "We did!"

Watt roots in the bag for the cigarettes "Here I am with my tongue hanging out for a smoke and you two come sauntering along the road as though you had all the time in the world. Ye better hurry on home with that shopping, cause Daddy's waiting for his supper."

When we get home, I hand Daddy his tobacco, and I think of my ringworm and wonder—was it the tobacco, the drink in his spit, or the DDT on the bandages that cured it?

No Santa

Santa Claus was supposed to come to us last night, but I was the only one who got anything. We all wrote to him and Mammy posted the letters. I was awake last night when Daddy came home and he and Mammy argued. She was telling him, "There's a great curse in that drink and McQuaid is worse to be giving it to you."

He kept saying, "Will you leave me alone, woman? For God's sake, I only had a few pints." He kept talking, but I couldn't make out what he was saying. He mumbled a lot, like Liam Mahon when Mrs. O'Kelly asked him if he had marbles in his mouth. He went to bed and I heard Mammy crying. When I woke this morning and looked under the bed there was nothing, and Santa hadn't come.

I went down to the kitchen and there in the middle of the floor were the new boots I asked for, with an apple inside one of them. There were two pieces of sticks sticking out of them like legs, and they were laced up with what looked like over twenty knots in them. Frank and Eddie got a ball and some sweets. Chris said he doesn't believe in Santa anyway. Anne was really disappointed and vexed. She says this is the first Christmas we didn't get some little thing. And what will we tell the other children at school when they ask us what we got? And she hopes Mrs O'Kelly doesn't ask us to write a composition on it like she did last year.

Teresa says, "That's exactly what Mrs. O'Kelly will do—especially if she hears about it. Well anyway," she adds, "we can always tell a bunch of lies like we always have to. Do yis remember the time when she asked me what I got from Santa Clause? And when I told her I got a big doll. She asked me to bring it in, as she would like to see it. She knew damn well it was a lie. Next day I had to tell another lie and say I lost it. Then she says, 'I feel sorry for yis.'"

Teresa says, "I can't wait till I'm old enough to go to England. There's nothing in this hell hole of a place but hunger, gossip, drink, and abuse."

I'm thinking to myself: I don't care because I have my new boots. Now if I could only undo all those knots.

My happiness is short lived because anytime there's something to be done they all say, "Let the one with the new boots do it." There's no fire and no turf in the shed, and only a few sticks left from what we gathered yesterday. Watt was supposed to get a load of turf from Pop Mahon, but he didn't get paid for some drains he cleaned, and he said he wouldn't ask for turf on credit.

Mammy says, "No, but you wouldn't mind getting cigarettes on credit."

Chris and I have to go for sticks. Daddy came home without any shopping. He was supposed to bring home a ham or turkey. That's what they were fighting about last night. He tried to tell Mammy he paid McQuaid for a turkey, but she told him she didn't believe it. She said, "If you paid him for a turkey, he would have sent it up here long ago."

We get the fire lit and the kettle boiled, and at least there's a cake of bread Mammy baked last evening, and some butter. We can fill up on that.

We've no money in the house, and Anne says even if there was, she's one that won't go to any shops on Christmas Day. Not if she was killed or dying in the ditch of hunger.

I picture Anne lying in the ditch and hope the rats don't bite her. People are beginning to go to First Mass, and Mammy and Daddy will sleep late as usual. Mammy says the bed is the warmest part of the house and it takes her out of her misery.

A group of tinkers have camped in the green, and I wonder if they're cold. The only fire they have is outside their tents. Mammy says at one time they were tinsmiths and made pots and pans, but all those things are now made in factories, and the tinkers have fallen on hard times. In fact, they're reduced to begging. I saw them make a bucket once, and all they had to use was a small hammer, what looked like scissors for cutting metal, and a small anvil half the size of the one in the forge. Some of them are good, and some not so good and steal from people. One woman named Powers comes to our door once a year. She tells Mammy if she can spare a sixpence fine, and if not she will pray for her anyway. Mammy says she's a decent woman.

One time Mammy was saving to buy clothes for Margaret's Confirmation and a tinker woman came to the door asking for money. Mammy said she didn't have any. The woman said, "Don't be afraid to wake the baby, Mrs. Burke, because I could put him to sleep with a blow of my breath."

Mammy was afraid of her and gave her all the money she'd hidden under Eddie. Mammy told Mrs.Crinegan the woman had supernatural powers and knew the money was hid under the baby.

"Ah! God help your head, Mrs. Burke," said Mrs. Crinegan, "sure your brain must be addled. Those people travel the length and breath of Ireland and it's a well-known fact that mothers hide money from drunken husbands under the baby."

"Ah! Yes, Mrs.Crinegan, but how would she know that I had a baby at my age?"

"Well, if you just ask, you'll find she had a word with someone at the crossroads before she came to you."

Mammy wasn't convinced, but she never did tell Daddy about it. Teresa wonders why they beg from those that have less than themselves.

By the time we get back with sticks for the fire, Watt is up and having his tea. He tells Mammy he'll kill one of the hens for dinner. "Sure," he says, "they're no good anyway and seldom lay an egg."

Mammy says, "Make sure you don't kill one that's laying."

"And pray tell how am I supposed to know which one is laying and which is not?"

She tells him to try them with your finger to see if there is an egg in them.

He says, "I will in my eye try them with my finger!"

We have six hens again, plus the cock and turkey. I'm glad he's not going to kill the cock as I had a lot of fun with him till he got too cowardly. I would swing the cock back and forth at the turkey till both of them got real mad, then I'd throw him at the turkey and they would fight each other. They fought well at first, till the turkey tore feathers out of the cock a few times and he wouldn't fight anymore. One day Mammy caught me at it. She gave me a right slap in the jaw and said, "How do you expect the turkey to lay and you teasing it all the time?"

Watt sharpens a knife with a scythe stone, goes out to the hen house, and cuts the head off a hen. When he comes in, he says it's the turkey he should have killed, because all it does is eat and he doubts it will ever lay an egg. Mammy tells him, "Take care you don't touch that turkey. That turkey will lay come spring." She tells Anne and I to pluck the hen while it's warm.

Anne says, "Let the one with the new boots do it."

Daddy shouts down, "Don't have me come down to you or you'll know what it's about."

We pluck the hen in the empty turf shed and it's nearly as big as a turkey. When we get it cleaned out, we can see there is no egg in it. Watt says it was too big and fat and lazy to lay eggs. Margaret says, "You mean it was too old; sure that hen has been there for donkeys years." We gather all the feathers and insides and bury them in the garden.

People are going home from First Mass. I'm trying to get ready for last Mass and Teresa is brushing feathers out of my jumper. My sleeves aren't as snotty as they used to be, because I finally learned to put my finger to one side of my nose and blow. I quit using my sleeve after Margaret told me my nose was all to one side from pulling my sleeve across it.

Chris has already left for Mass, as he is serving. He served at a wedding last week and got sixpence. He saves all his money and won't even buy sweets. He says he's saving to go to Butlin's Holiday camp. Anne says he's so tight he squeaks when he walks. I never heard him squeak.

Mass is said quickly this morning. The priest must be in a hurry to get to breakfast. I can't go to Communion because I had bread and butter this morning and stole sugar from the bowl. You can't go to Communion with a sin on your soul.

Fridays are fast days and days of abstinence and we can't eat meat. I think it doesn't matter to us, because we seldom have meat anyway. Teresa says every day in our house is a fast day lately.

When I get home Watt has found some carrots and parsnips in the garden. We have potatoes that I dug up yesterday, along with some onions. Teresa says she'll make dumplings. Chris gives two pence to Frank and Eddie for Christmas; Mammy says that's very nice of him. I hope he doesn't take it back later like he did with me one time. We all teased him about that. "Give a thing and take it back. God will ask you where's that, you'll say you don't know and God will send you down below."

The house is nice and warm, and while we got few presents, I am happy with my new boots. And food wise it isn't too bad after all.

The Wren Boys

The day after Christmas is a time of fun and laughter. In our part of the country it's called Wren Day. People with musical talent get together in groups and go hunting the wren.

Seán Rogers, Patsy Rogers, Pat Shanley, Liam Tormey, and Joe Burke make up the best group from Moyvore. They dress up with disguises on their faces to look like clowns and other creatures. All five of them can entertain in some way or another. Seán Rodgers plays the mouth organ, and dances at the same time. Patsy Rodgers sings. Joe Burke plays the Bodhrán (drum) and step dances. Pat Shanley strums the Jew's harp and sings, and Liam Tormey plays the tin whistle.

It's nine o'clock on a frosty morning and they gather at the crossroads for their final practice. They go around in a circle and chant, "The wren, the wren, the king of all birds. St. Stephen's day he was caught in the furz. Up with the kettle and down with the pan. Give us a penny to bury the wren. If you haven't got a penny a ha'penny will do. If you haven't got a ha'penny then God bless you." They use this chant when approaching a house and if they hear the words, "You're welcome," they go in and break into music, song and dance. They will entertain that house for about fifteen minutes, sometimes more, depending on what is put into the hat they pass around.

They cover all the Ballymore area during the day, and return to Moyvore in the evening. They come to our house and dance and sing and play music for nearly an hour. They will finish up the day in one of the pubs in the village, entertaining the customers.

"And you know, Mrs. Burke," says Seán Rodgers, "we went into one house and played and danced for twenty minutes and they never gave us a feckin penny. So didn't some of the boys see a currant cake cooling on the windowsill and we snatched it and rode to Rooney's of High Street in Ballymore where we bought lemonade and the five of us ate the whole thing."

Mammy says, "Wasn't it mean of them not to give yis anything, but isn't it a sin to steal?"

Seán says, "It is, missus, but when dealing with people as mean as they were, it would be a bigger sin if we didn't."

One of the wren boys is standing by the door doing nothing. Daddy looks at him and says, "What are you doing back in this house? And didn't I tell you never to set foot in this house again." At this point Joe takes off his disguise only to show us that it isn't Joe, but Pat Shanley. He says to Daddy, "Are you talking to me?"

Daddy says, "Sorry, Pat, I mistook you for someone else." Apparently Joe and Pat Shanley had switched clothes at the crossroads.

Teresa is asked to perform, and she sings, "If I were a blackbird I'd whistle and sing, and I would follow the ship that my true love sailed in."

Patsy Rodgers tells her, "You've a grand voice and it's no wonder they call you the thrush."

Mammy is persuaded to give a recitation and she begins.

"A man whose name was Johnny Sands
Had married Betty Haig
All though she gave him gold and land
He proved a terrible plague.

Then said he I'll drown myself
The river runs below
Said she pray do you silly elf
Sure I wished it long ago

For fear that I should courage lack
And try to save my life
Pray tie my hands behind my back
I will replied his wife

She tied them hard as you may think
And when securely done
Said she now stand upon the brink
And I'll prepare to run

All down the hill his loving bride
She ran with all her might
To push him in he stepped aside
And she fell in of course

Oh splashing dashing like a fish
She cried save me Johnny Sands
I can't my dear though much I wish
For you have tied my hands."

She gets a big round of applause. And Seán Rodgers says, "Fair
play to ya, missus. I knew you could do it; sure good breeding will
always break out in people. Now Joe Burke, that's putting it up to ya.
Surely you can't let the missus get away with that. You'll have to
give us a bit of a song, if only a few verses just to bring balance to the
situation."
    They all say, "Come on, Joe, we know you can do it!"
    "And I wouldn't mind," says Mammy, "but he got prizes for
singing years ago." Daddy gives in and breaks into song.

"It's in this world I gained my knowledge
And for it I had to pay
Although I never went to college
I have heard the poet's say.

Life is like a mighty river
Flowing on from day to day
Men and vessel launch upon it
Off times wrecked and cast away

Many is the noble-hearted fellow
Many is the noble-minded man
Finds himself in waters shallow
Please assist him if you can

So do your best for one another
Make of life a pleasant dream
Help a weary and a worn brother
Pulling hard against the stream"

There comes another round of applause. "Be Janey, Joe," says Liam Tormey, "you still have it." Daddy seems pleased and everyone looks happy as the wren boys head toward the gate. Seán Rodgers is saying to no one in particular. "This is a great day, boys, and it's only beginning."

Chapter Seven

Boarding School

Margaret comes home from the Convent of Mercy in Ballymahon at the end of each term. She's always studying for one exam or another. Teresa complains that she takes up the whole bed with her books and stays up half the night reading with a candle. She declares that if she herself studied that much she'd become a solicitor at least.

Margaret tells her, "Jealousy will get you nowhere," and continues her studies. She has a tea chest turned upside down beside the bed to act as a table. We got the empty chest from Shaw's. The tea chests are about eighteen inches wide and twenty inches high, with silver lining on the inside. We were using it to hold sticks and turf, but now that Margaret has it, we just put the turf and sticks on the floor behind the kitchen door.

Mammy says, "If Margaret doesn't succeed, then it won't be for the lack of trying. I've never seen any of yis put in as much effort into studies as she does."

Mona Burns asks Anne, "What is Margaret going to be when she finishes school?"

Anne said, "She's going to be a teacher."

Mona huffed at her, "Anne Burke, will you not be making a dog's arse out of your mouth? No one, but no one, has ever become a teacher out of Moyvore, and what makes you think that Maggie Burke is any different? And what's more, Daddy says there's never been a scholarship since Mrs. O'Kelly took over that school."

Anne says, "I can only tell you what she told me. Take it or leave it."

One time Mona was asked to write a composition about the river Shannon and all she could write was one sentence "The river is very long with a wide bottom."

Mammy sends us to ask Joe for money for food, but he seldom has any. He's living with Donald Rush and I think he only gets cigarette money from him. He quit his job with the land commission when he had words with the foreman. Although the foreman told Joe to forget it and come back to work, Joe told him, "Stick your job where Biddy hid the rent."

After that, Joe went to work for Bob Mearse, but soon quit him also. As the story goes, he was ploughing a field at the back of the green with two Bay horses that had been idle all winter. They were wild and hard to manage. As a result, the opening scribe was crooked and, when he saw it, Bob said, "By God, Joe, if I wanted it ploughed in circles I would have started you around a hill." Joe got vexed, threw the reins on the horses, and walked off. Bob shouted at him to at least take home the horses and Joe said, "Take them home your f——ng self."

Joe had the usual amount of trouble at school as a boy. One time he was on the roof of the lavatory near our house in the village taking a pee when he heard shouts coming from inside. It was Mrs. O'Kelly. There were rusty holes in the roof and the pee was running down in on top of her.

Next day she was beating Joe on the head with the roller from the school map. Tom stepped in and asked her if she'd like to try it on him. He grabbed the roller and broke it across his knees. Mrs. O'Kelly was a bit afraid of Tom, or so it was said. Tom was strong and stocky as a young fellow. He even cut turf for the land commission at sixteen—he told them he was twenty-one.

Even with Tom's intervention, Joe spent a week at home in bed with headaches.

Halloween

Halloween was usually a night of trickery in our village. Many of the local homes had their gates taken and hidden or a cart wheel might go missing and be found down the road the next day. Such mischief was traditional.

This particular Halloween night some of the lads got creative and took the wheels off Joe Kenny's cart and brought them into his kitchen. Then they brought the cart in, put the wheels back on and yoked the pony up to the cart inside the kitchen. When Joe got home from having his few pints, he thought he was going crazy or that the Fairies had cursed him.

Another fine trick was orchestrated at the nine-foot gate between Shaw's pub and Tormey's yard. The shafts of Jim Mullin's cart were pushed through the gate and the ass yoked up on the other side. When Jim came out from the pub he stood in amazement, scratching his head. He was heard to say, " I don't know how you got in to it, but you'll get out of it."

Later on that night, some of Tom's friends gathered outside Egan's pub and told Tom that they'd gotten James Ward's gate and wanted to leave it up in Ballymore, but they had no way to do it. Delighted to be in on the trickery, Tom said, "I can do it and only I can do it, as I'm the only one strong enough."

He got on the best bike available and they loaded the Iron Gate on his back. Off he went riding the four miles to Ballymore in the dark. At Low Street, he dumped the gate. He returned to great praise and back slapping. Then they all had some drinks to celebrate their evening of trickery.

The next day, we woke to find our gate missing. We later found it at Low Street in Ballymore where Tom had left it. The trick was on him.

The most serious Halloween trick was revealed when James Kane, the biggest farmer around Moyvore, discovered that his tractor was missing. There was no laughing when the Gardaí Síochána came out from Mullingar and made the usual inquiries. Although it was found a few miles away, they never discovered who took it.

That year just about spelled the end of Halloween as we knew it. Smiler Cormack voiced his disgust at the whole situation saying, "The whole damn country has gone too civilized and uppity to be wholesome."

Lamb of God

"And the poor auld devil was just laying there looking up at me with his sad eyes. You know I almost cried. I wanted to say, 'Here I am Benny, I'll save you,' but I knew I couldn't."

George Scally was telling us about a pet lamb he used to own. He got the lamb when two drovers with a dog were driving a herd of sheep from Ballymahon to Mullingar. One of the sheep lambed near Scally's house and they gave the lamb to George, as they couldn't take it with them. Mrs. Scally gave them tea and they went their way.

George nursed and cared for the lamb every day till it grew to full size. One day Gus Kenny pulled up in his car and took the lamb to his butcher stall.

George followed him there and saw his pet lamb being killed. He told us how Gus Kenny put a knife in behind his ear and twisted it till the lamb bled to death as he held it down with his knees. George said, "I wanted to tell him, 'No, you can't kill my lamb!' but I knew I couldn't. Daddy sold him the lamb and he told me a deal is a deal and the lamb isn't yours anymore." George's story reminds me of a poem Mammy taught me.

Lamb of God

All in the April evening,
April airs were abroad,
the sheep with their little lambs
passed me by on the road.

The sheep with their little lambs
passed me by on the road;
all in the April evening
I thought on the Lamb of God.
The Lambs were weary, and crying
with a weak, human cry.
I thought on the Lamb of God
going meekly to die.

Up in the blue, blue mountains
dewy pastures are sweet;
rest for the little bodies,
rest for the little feet,

But for the Lamb of God,
up on the hill-top green,
only a cross of shame
two stark crosses between.

All in the April evening,
April airs were abroad,
I saw the sheep with their lambs,
And I thought on the Lamb of God.

Some of the school children are shocked by George's tale, especially the girls.

Kenny's butcher's stall has always seemed a cold place to me. It is housed in a cement building with a v-shaped asbestos roof and double doors in a big yard behind Tormey's house. Inside, a bench runs from one wall to the other and a round ring in the wall is used to pull in the haltered animal to be killed. A rope from the haltered animal goes through the ring and one man pulls on it while another pushes the animal from behind. Once the bullock is pulled inside and his head is tight to the wall, the men tie the rope to a hook at the door.

Seán Rodgers works part time for Gus Kenny and does most of the killing. First they use a lump hammer to stun the animal. And then they use a pole axe to kill it. This is like a regular axe with a round, pointed spike on one end. They swing it like an axe and drive the spike in at the back of the head. When the bullock falls, its hind legs are coupled together with clamps Daddy made. A block and tackle fixed to an iron beam in the roof is then used to hang the bullock for butchering.

Gus Kenny drinks a lot and once I saw him have to hit the bullock three or four times with the pole axe before it fell. I'm glad that Seán Rodgers does most of the killing.

The Measles

The sun is shining and there is no one home except Mammy and myself. Everyone else has headed off for the match in Garrison's field, where Moyvore is playing Miltown for the medals. And here am I am in bed, with the measles they gave me. Chris and Frank got over them over a week ago after staying in bed for three days.

My body is covered with little red spots and I feel sick, but I'm determined not to miss that football match. I wait till Mammy is real quiet and I peek down in the kitchen. She isn't there, and the door to her room is closed. I know I can't open the front door or she'll hear me, so I find my britches under the bed and sneak out the window.

The gate is open, so I don't have to worry about it squeaking and waking Mammy. I hurry up the Mullingar Road as far as Scally's, glad to see no one there. I don't want to run into George, because I wouldn't be able to fight him, and he'd tell everyone I was too cowardly. By the time I reach Garahan's gate, I can hear cheering way off in the field, and the gate is closed over and tied with a chain. I decide it's easier to climb over than try to undo the chain.

When I get to the top of the gate, I feel dizzy and light headed, the ground looks as though it's miles away. I start to shake and cold sweat breaks out on my forehead. I climb down and sit on a rock that fell off the stone wall. I realize I can't go any further, so I decide to start for home. I walk only short way when Nicholas Rooney comes along with a pony and trap.

He opens the little door at the back of the trap and says, "Get in, young Burke." The minute I get in he looks at me and he asks, "Do you have the measles?" I tell him I do, and then he asks me, "Does your mother know you're out?"

I say, "No, she told me to stay in bed, but I got out the window to go to the match."

"Oh!" he says, "that's right! Sure they're playing the finals today. I don't follow it myself, but I did hear them talking about it." He's a nice man and always well dressed. I heard Daddy saying he was in America and came home and bought a farm. Sometimes he comes to the forge, and if I am pulling the bellows, he throws pennys up at the ceiling when I'm not looking and says, "By Janey, it's raining money again." Other than Daddy, he's the only one that ever does that.

We get to the crossroads and as Mr. Rooney lets me out, he calls after me, "Maybe you can get back in without being noticed, and if you say nothing, neither will I."

I say, "Thanks, Mr. Rooney." Luckily the gate and the window are still open. I climb in the window, get into bed, and fall asleep. I dream about lambs.

Hunger Strike

Daddy is in bed sick. He's been in bed ever since Mammy and him had a big fight. He pushed past her and stormed up to the room. After awhile he came down and they went out to the gate and stayed there talking for a long time. He put his arm around her and they walked around the house and stopped at the front barrel of water, looking in at something. I wondered what they were looking at, and as soon as they moved away I went to the barrel and looked in but I couldn't see anything. I could see right to the bottom of it, even the few inches of tar left inside when we got it from the council. I just didn't know what to make of it. But I did know it was better than hearing them argue.

Inside again, she gave him tea and bread and butter, and he said a few things needed doing in the forge. He said he'd be home about six for the supper. He didn't get home till after eleven o'clock. Mammy kept sending us to the crossroads to see if there was any sign of him. He'd been doing this a lot more often since Tom left.

Watt talked to John McQuaid about it and he agreed to talk with Daddy and try to get him to go home at a decent hour. Daddy got vexed with McQuaid and told him he would take his business elsewhere. He started going to Egan's pub and taking other customers with him. He'd often done this in the past, and soon McQuaid would coax him back again.

When Daddy finally got home that evening, a horse and cart stopped at the gate and Watt had to go out and help him into the house. Mammy said, "Your dinner has been there waiting since six o'clock. Not that you care, because you just don't care about anything. Not about your wife, not about your house or family. All you care about is that rotten drink."

I could hear this in bed. I didn't think Mammy would ever talk to him like that. That was over a week ago, and Daddy hasn't eaten since. He just lies in bed, and sometimes I hear him moan. I peep around the door to his room and he seems to be asleep. I tip toe over to the bed and I can see his teeth, and the gaps where some of them are missing. They're all black and rotten looking and his face is covered with beard. I wonder why he never brushes his teeth.

The dentist started coming to our school last year. He gave all the children toothbrushes, and a talk on how to use them. Mammy bought a tin of toothpaste. It's like a polish tin and the toothpaste is pink. We all use the same tin, and it's worn down in the middle from our brushes so we can see the shiny bottom of the tin. I don't like being the last one to use it, because by then it's all suds from the others. When Margaret comes home from boarding school, she says it isn't healthy to be using the same tin of toothpaste. She has her own for school, and when she forgot to bring it home one time she took out a piece from the side of our tin with a knife and it left a hole that took a long time to wear out.

Mammy doesn't brush her teeth much either, but hers are not all black like Daddy's. I think it must be because she doesn't drink or smoke a pipe like Daddy or Rosie Crinegan. Teresa is upset about Daddy being in bed and says, "This is just great; all we need now is for Daddy to die on hunger strike."

Mammy eventually sends for Tom who tries coaxing Daddy to eat. "Ah! Come on, sure that's only an auld cod of a way of going on. Sure you have to eat. What do you think you can do, just lie there in bed till you die?"

There is little response from Daddy except a very low, "Maybe so."

Then Tom says, "There's a lot of work needs doing in the forge. I can help out, but I can't do it all on my own, and some people won't come in to get work done if they know you aren't there. Here, I'll leave this bit of mashed potatoes and egg on the stool and you can eat it when you feel up to it. I'll come up to see you this evening."

Tom comes down and Mammy and him are sitting by the fire whispering. Mammy tells us to leave the house. There is only the five of us. Chris is on the bog catching turf for Tom Cormack and Seán is with Mick Brennan. Anne asks me, "Do you think Daddy will die?"

I say, "I don't know." I want to say I don't care, only I'm not sure whether I do or not. If he dies, he won't get to beat me anymore, and we won't have to watch out for him all the time. I feel I'm free since he took to the bed and doesn't ask us to do anything. On the other hand, I don't like to see Mammy upset and crying, and if he dies maybe she'll cry all the time. Then I think if he started eating and got better and stayed in bed, wouldn't it be just great.

I ask Anne what she thinks about that idea and she says, "It is just about what a small mind would think of. How can you stay in bed if you aren't sick? Sure if we could do that, all we would ever need is a bed." Then she says, "I saw Mammy crying several times when she thought no one was looking."

Frank says, "So did I." I feel sorry for Frank, because he's not sure what is going on, and neither am I. Eddie is too young to care. When Eddie was born, Daddy asked Mammy if she thought he would ever see him reared.

When I really think about Daddy dying on hunger strike, I get a kind of a shiver on me, and my belly feels nearly like it did when we ate the red haws. Or the time I had a feed of crab apples down in Bob Mearse's field but a different kind of a feeling. The five of us are standing in the turf shed to stay out of the rain.

Anne asks, "Do yis notice that we don't have to empty the poe near as often since Daddy got sick?"

Then she says, "We might as well go for the water and get it over with, so we won't have to do it this evening."

I go in for the bucket and Mammy and Tom are still sitting by the fire drinking tea. Tom has the cup in his hands between his knees with his thumbs over the top of it. I wonder is he trying to break it or keep it warm. I like Tom because he's gentle, and never beats us like Daddy and Watt, and he makes Mammy feel good. Teresa often says he's the best of the whole lot of them, and why couldn't it have been Watt that had to leave instead of Tom?

Anne says, "Maybe Nanny Molloy didn't want Watt. And besides how do you know that Tom won't be like Daddy when he gets older?"

Inside the house, I hear Mammy asking Tom, "Do you think we should send for the doctor?"

He responds, "Sure what good will that do? The minute the doctor hears he hasn't eaten for eight days he'll say he can't do anything. Now if we could get him eating a little bit for a few days, then we could get the doctor. You leave it to me, Mammy, and I bet ya I'll have him eating by this evening."

Mammy spots me and tells me get out and not be listening to grown up talk. I fill the kettle with the water from the bucket and pour the rest in the washbasin. This is the first time Tom has been in the house since he left to marry Nanny Molloy. Still worried, Mammy says, "He was skin and bone already without this, and there's work in the forge to be done and no one to do it."

Tom says, "Don't worry about the forge. I'll take care of it, and wait till you see, I'll get Daddy to eat too."

When Watt heard about it, he said, "Sure he'll take care of the forge. He's been trying to get back in there ever since he got ran off."

Tom does get Daddy to eat, but it takes a few more days. He comes up from the forge twice a day, coaxing him till finally he gives in and eats some mashed potatoes and egg. Doctor Joyce gives him a bottle of tonic and a bottle of red stuff for his stomach.

The Cow

Watt has bought a cow—a young shorthorn heifer in calf. He was cleaning drains for some farmer down in Milltown who asked him to wait three months for his money, so he made a deal to buy the heifer. The price was fourteen pounds, and the farmer owed him twelve. Watt borrowed two pounds from Jim Finn to make up the difference and he went down and paid the farmer in full.

The heifer calved that night and had a little white-faced heifer calf. He had to borrow Smiler Cormack's ass and cart to go and pick up the calf. We were all waiting for him as he came up the Chapel Road, leading the ass and cart with the mother following behind.

Everyone has an opinion about that cow. Mrs. Crinegan claims a shorthorn cow is no good to give milk. Seán Rodgers says if a shorthorn cow's first calf is a heifer, then all her calves will be heifers, and heifer calves aren't worth near as much as bull calves. Even Daddy gets in on the act. He says he was talking to Pat Donohue, who said he knew that heifer and she had the makings of a fine cow.

Teresa says, "Fair play to Watt; at least it's more than anyone else has ever done around here." Pat Shanley claims that although a shorthorn won't give as much milk as a Kerry blue or a whiteface, the milk is a lot richer. He says, "James Kane is the biggest farmer around and would have nothing only shorthorns, so what does that tell you?"

Jim Finn tells Watt not to listen to any of them saying, "You made a good deal and that's that. Let them all go straight to hell, they and their opinions."

Watt says he knows one thing for sure—it's better to have a cow about the place than to be beggin for a jug of milk every day. Seán looks at him in a knowing way and says, "Maybe it's even better than having a goat around the place too." This is in reference to the time that our goat disappeared after eating Watt's cabbage plants. Where it got to no one seemed to know. It was rumored later that the goat was killed and the skin used to make a Bodhrán so the boys could go hunting the wren.

Anyway, we all love the cow and we've sectioned off part of the shed for her and the calf. We won't be able to use the milk for a week, as it will be too strong. At this stage it's called beestings. Mammy makes a mash for the cow in the basin from potatoes, turnips and Indian meal. That cow has become such a pet that she nearly comes in the kitchen. We bought a second hand churn from Mick Brennan and we start saving the cream to make butter. We milk the cow twice a day. She grazes on the side of the road, and we have to go looking for her in the evenings after school. It was easy to find her at first, as she would never stray too far from her calf, but after Watt sold the calf to pay bills, she began straying all over the place.

Sometimes we have to walk several miles to find her. One time we caught two tinkers at her, one was holding her and the other milking her. They ran off when they saw us. They must have got most of her milk because she didn't give much that evening.

There's great excitement when we make the first butter; it tastes so good we nearly eat it like ice cream. Mrs. Crinegan showed Mammy how to make it, and how to paddle it with the clappers. They are like two wooden paddles with grooves in them, used to firm the butter and get the milk and salt out of it.

Mrs. Crinegan told us the story of when Paddy Allan's wife was in bed with the flu and Paddy was making the butter in the kitchen. He was clapping the butter over the pot he had just boiled for the pigs. She shouted down to him, "Clap it, Paddy Allan. Clap it!" Just then, the butter fell and he shouted back to her, "You can clap your arse now, it's in the pig's pot."

We churn butter every eight to ten days, and we feel rich. One evening sitting at the fire with our bellies full, Mammy teaches us a poem about the friendly cow.

The friendly cow all red and white
I love with all my heart.
She gives me cream with all her might
to eat with apple tart.

She wanders looking here and there
and yet she cannot stray.
All in the pleasant open air
the pleasant light of day.

Everyone thinks it's a shame that Mammy didn't get a chance to continue in school as she would have been a great teacher. She is always telling us stories, reciting poems, or reading when she can get the books. That's rare since, the bus used as a borrowing library only comes to our village once a month.

Cut Wrist

The fence at the end of our house has a round wooden railing on top. Watt built it to keep us out of the little garden he dug to sow winter cabbage . The railing is about four inches thick and we use it as a greasy pole like the one we saw at the Abbeyshrule sports. We try to walk along the top of it without falling off. Because there's no water underneath it where we could fall off and drown, we use a blindfold to make it harder. I'm halfway across on my second go when I fall off and cut my wrist on a piece of a rusty polish tin. When I stand up, the blood is pumping out of my wrist like a fountain.

By the time I reach the house, blood is going all over my clothes and the floor. Mammy just stands there looking white in the face not knowing what to do. Margaret urgently tears a sheet into strips and starts to wrap them around my wrist. The more bandages she puts on, the more it seems that the blood comes through. She tells Mammy we should get the doctor. Mammy says, "We can't get the doctor as we have no bike to go for him, and your Daddy is really busy in the forge."

Teresa speaks up, saying Nanny Rooney is home from England and she's a nurse and will know what to do. Teresa then heads off for Nanny Rooney. When Nanny arrives, she puts more bandages on my wrist. I'm not feeling too good about Nanny helping me being as the last time I saw Nanny Rooney was when Bernie Casey died in front of her house, and she didn't seem to be able to do much for him. Nanny finally tells Mammy that she should get me to the doctor, as I could bleed to death.

When she leaves, I think to myself, some feckin' help you are Nanny Rooney. Thanks for nothing. Then I get to thinking that if she is a nurse and can't stop the bleeding, then maybe it can't be stopped. Maybe she didn't want to stay and see me bleed to death. I look down at my wrist and the bandages are all slimy and sticky from my blood. My wrist is nearly as big as a small football.

Everyone is getting upset at all the blood. Eddie faints and they have to carry him to bed. It's then that Margaret says, "That's it! I'm sending for Daddy." She tells Frank, "Run as fast as you can down to the forge and get Daddy to come home."

At this stage, I don't know if I'm more scared of getting a beating from Daddy's leather belt or bleeding to death. They keep telling me to hold up my arm and not let it be dropping so the blood won't flow out. It's getting real heavy and I have to use my other arm to help hold it up. They make a sling and put it over my shoulder, which takes the weight off it. My jumper and britches is all red and sticky with blood, and I think maybe I won't have to go to the hospital. Sure how can I go to the hospital with bloody clothes? Anyway, I don't want to go there, because that's where people die. Bernie Casey died and they said he was in his thirties.

By the time Daddy gets home I'm real dizzy and seeing two and three of everything. Although I know full well that we only have one tongs, I see two of them. I know it must be my eyes that aren't right.

"What happened here?" Daddy demands.

Mammy says, "Pat was climbing the fence and fell and cut his wrist."

Now I know I'm really in for it. He warned us a week ago to stay away from there. Then I think if he doesn't stop this bleeding, I'll be dead anyway and he can beat me all he wants.

He takes my arm from the sling and asks, "Who did this?"

Mammy says, "Margaret and Nanny Rooney."

"I thought you said that Rooney girl was a nurse? Well if she is, I'm afraid she'd better go back and do some more training."

He takes off the sling and presses both thumbs on my arm above the elbow till his fingernails are white. He tells Margaret to take off all the bandages, and I watch them as they pile up on the floor in layers of red and white. There are all shades of red and brown on the bandages.

Daddy then puts a half crown on the wound and holds it tight while Margaret puts on new bandages. The bleeding has almost stopped, and at least it's only coming through the first few layers. Then I think that maybe all my blood is gone and that's how I'm going to die. Daddy finishes putting on the rest of the bandages and tells me to go to bed for awhile.

I lay in bed with my arm in the air to make sure I don't fall asleep, in case it's the last thing I do. I don't remember when I fell off to sleep, but the next thing I know it's the next morning. I feel weak and lightheaded. When Mammy sees me she says, "You look as though you saw a ghost."

Teresa nods saying, "He does look a bit pale."

Anne laughs and says, "That's it then. We'll call him Paleen."

I think to myself, God, does she ever stop with her big mouth? Here I am nearly dying and she still wants to call me names. But still I'm comforted by the fact that she looks happy that I didn't die. And if she won't admit it, then why was she crying when they couldn't stop the bleeding? I bet she thinks I didn't see her, but I did.

I carry those bandages and the half crown for over a week, till Sunday, when Daddy took them off. He put the half crown in his pocket, and went off to the pub.

I didn't bleed to death, and I didn't get a beating. All in all, I fared pretty well. As for Daddy—well, he probably saved my life.

Chapter Eight

Sam Connaughton

The farmers prayed for good weather and God heard them. The weather has been fine for the past month with not a drop of rain. Now the land is bone dry and starting to crack, so the eejits are praying for rain. Daddy reckons there should be a God just for farmers—one who'd give them perfect weather all the time. "Yes," he says, "a special weather God for farmers. Then, of course, the days might be too long or too short and they'd need a special God for that too. It just goes to prove you can't please everyone all of the time."

Chris and I are delivering a telegram to Sam Connaughton. Chris got a part time job from the post office. There aren't many telegrams to deliver anymore and he thinks it's because more people have cars and bikes and they want to pick up their own mail. On the way to Connaughton's, we see Pat Scally filling in the holes on the Ballymore Road with his pony and cart.

It's a fine day which is a good thing because it's much easier on our feet when the roads are dry. When it rains, the water washes away the fine sand and leaves the rough stones sticking out which hurt our bare feet. Along the road, bushes are loaded with blackberries and haws. We eat our feed of them as we go. There are gooseberries too, but they're hard to get at because of the nettles and briers.

We spot Lilly Rodgers coming toward us with a bundle of yellow cowslips she just picked. She asks us, "Do yis have any fags?" Before we can answer she says, "Ah, sure yis wouldn't, sure yis are too young to smoke." Chris confirms that we don't and, once we're out of her hearing, he tells me she picks butts of cigarettes off the road, rolls them in a piece of newspaper, and smokes them. We think she's a bit daft.

Everywhere we look, there are bright colors. Dandelions dot the fields with yellow, and the fuzzy thistle tops seem ready to launch in the breeze. The smell of fresh cut grass wafts from the trams of hay scattered in some fields. Other fields are ripe with crops of wheat or oats waiting to be harvested.

When we reach a gate, we climb it and look out into other fields watching the sheep. Chris calls them woolly jumpers and I laugh at the name.

On our way again, we pass the first house on the Ballymore Road, where James and Mrs. Finn live. Paddy White lived there before them. There is a man's flannel shirt stretched across the front window as a make-do curtain. James Finn is an odd man who seems to be always humming and talking to himself. It's hard to hear what he's saying because he makes a plopping sound when he opens and closes his mouth. His lower lip goes in over his gums and his upper lip comes down over it.

Chris says James Finn reminds him of a man he once saw in the pictures in Ballymahon called Gabby Hayes. I've never been to the pictures. Chris says it costs nine pence to get in to see them. He says there is a big screen with a lot of people and horses on it.

I ask him, "What's a screen?" and he tells me, "It's like a white painted wall."

I don't quite understand it, but I want him to think I'm smart, so I say nothing. But I do wonder to myself if that Gabby Hayes fellow will still be there when I finally go to the pictures.

As we continue on the road, I think about Sam Connaughton. He's a handy man and jack-of-all-trades for the local farmers. He's also a bonesetter and acts as a vet for those who can't afford the real vet from Mullingar, or Ballymahon. One time when I was weeding turnips for the Daltons, Sam came and castrated a suck pig with his penknife. When he finished, he wiped the knife across his britches and put it in his pocket. Sometime later I saw him peel and eat an apple with the same knife.

He usually has a dribble from his mouth that runs down his chin onto his coat and waistcoat. The front of his clothes are shiny black like the sleeves of my jumper. People say he never gets wet from the rain because the shiny dribble keeps him waterproof.

Mammy told us that he was once a county councilor elected by the people when he and Daddy were active in the I.R.A. (Irish Republican Army). She said, "What a pity he let himself go like that, and I wouldn't mind, but he had every chance in the world."

Some of the local lads liked to play tricks on Sam. One time when Sam had workers cutting turf on the bog, he decided to make pancakes for them as there was no bread to be got. He spent hours trying to fry those pancakes but he just couldn't get them to cook. Apparently, some of the lads had added a lot of white lime to the flour. He would've been there six days 'til Sunday and they never would've cooked.

Chris tells me that he will get six pence for delivering the telegram to Sam and has promised to give me two pence for going with him. He's never offered me anything before, so I think he must be afraid of Sam's dog. All farmers have dogs.

We get to an iron gate with two big stone piers on each side. The gate opens into a field that has a boreen (small road) along the side of a fence. A short way along the boreen is Sam Connaughton's place— a slated cottage surrounded by stone walls. Beside it is a turf shed that has three poles across the opening to keep the cows and calves out. A cow and several calves graze in the yard which is covered in cow shite. We're lucky that it's dry today so we can easily step around it. As we enter, the dogs start barking and a woman comes out waving a broom at them and saying, "Down outa dat." Upon seeing Chris, she calls to him, "Hello Bunny."

Chris has been called Bunny since he went to buy a penny bun in the shop. The shopkeeper in Shaw's said, "There's a penny bun for a Bunny," and from there on the name stayed with him. He didn't thank the shopkeeper for her trouble.

Pointing to me, the woman asks, "And which one of you is this?"

Chris says, "That's Paidin, ma'am."

"And is he the youngest?"

"No, two are younger than him."

"I see. Well, come inside the house and I'll give you some nice tea and bread. I have no jam, but I have some nice country butter. Ye must be famished after that long walk." We follow her through the half door and there's a chicken standing on the table picking at the bread. She swipes at it with the broom and, with a loud squawk, it flies out over the half door.

Mrs. Connaughton has a good fire burning and the kettle is boiling. A slab of bacon hangs from the ceiling, and hanging each side of it are two fly strips covered with black flies. She sees me looking at them and says, "Them old fly strips are nearly useless, sure they barely last a week in this weather before they fill up, and the Devil himself wouldn't keep the flies out."

As we sit at the table by the window, I notice that there are some sacks across the bottom rung. I think it must be a bed for the small terrier. Mrs. Connaughton tells us she lets the small dog in the house, but not the big one that's half greyhound. After the tea has drawn, Mrs. Connaughton takes the lid off the teapot and begins to pour the tea from the top of the teapot. She explains that the spout is stuffed from lime and won't pour properly anymore. Then she gives us two big slices of bread with butter spread on a half-inch thick. The butter smells funny and has green streaks through it.

Chris and I look at each other, but we dare not say a word. When Chris tries to give his to the dog, she sees him and says, "Don't do that, Bunny! It will only spoil him and he'll always be begging."

When she isn't looking, I scrape the butter off my bread with my fingers and stuff it up under the table. After forcing myself to eat a little piece of the bread, I nearly retch. Meanwhile, Chris has stuffed his in his britches pocket where it starts to melt with the heat of the fire. Finally, Mrs. Connaughton gives him the sixpence and we start to leave.

Outside, the big dog starts licking Chris's leg and britches. Mrs. Connaughton is amazed and says, "That dog really likes you, Bunny. I've never seen him be so friendly to anyone before." It took all I had to keep a straight face and not burst out laughing.

On the way home, I have great fun teasing Chris about it. That is until he threatens not to give me my two pence. He then tells me the sacks under the table were covering the latest pig Sam had killed. The pig's carcass was being salted there. We both thought how lucky we were that she didn't offer to fry bacon for us.

Death Pays a Visit

Daddy comes in the door and shakes the rainwater off his clothes. He stamps his shoes on the floor to get rid of the water running down from his black topcoat. When he takes off his tweed cap and swings it in an arc down by his side, a spray off water causes ashes to rise from the fire. He leans with his elbow against the wall over the fireplace. He's unusually quiet and pale. Mammy comes over to help him undo the buttons of his coat, and then she hangs it on the nail at the back of the door. Daddy then sits at the fire warming his hands, stretching them toward the flames. His whole body shudders as a shiver passes through him.

Nobody speaks as Mammy hands him a cup of tea. He brings the cup to his mouth and his hands are shaking. The bones in them stick out like small blue tree branches. His cheek bones are like two wrist knuckles and his jaws seem to be pushed into his mouth. We all know that he's been to see the surgeon in Mullingar. We're desperate to find out how it went. Finally, Mammy asks him, "What did the doctor say?"

He waits a bit longer, takes one hand off the cup, and then points to his stomach saying, "You have an ulcer there, Joe, and I don't like it."

"And what else did he say? Is he going to admit you to the hospital?"

Daddy responds, "No Breenie, leastways not yet. But he said he might have to send me to Dublin for an operation. He won't know till he gets the results of the x-rays."

He starts to cough, and a dribble comes from his nose that he wipes with the back of his hand. Daddy's been to see Doctor Joyce every week for the past four months, but now he can't ride the bike that far, so the doctor comes to see him twice a week. We aren't allowed in the house while the doctor's there. He gives Daddy the same two bottles of medicine, only more often. Daddy says the medicine is good for nothing, and the pains in his stomach have only gotten worse.

Later on, a woman comes to our house, the same woman who came the night Eddie was born. Anne said she peeked in the room and saw Daddy lying on his back on the floor. The woman kept putting a hot glass on his stomach. Teresa tells me it is called cupping, an old remedy to ease the pain. We hear him moaning in bed a lot of the time.

The past couple of weeks he's been walking to the forge, until it became too much for him. He has a favorite hen called Pluckeen that would wait for him on Mearse's stonewall and follow him home around the crossroads. Seán Rogers says it's not natural for a hen to do that—a dog or a cat maybe, but not a hen. She had chicks one time and he threw her a piece of bread that she broke up for them, and he said, "You're like every other old foolish mother of your sort."

Our dog Spot always follows him wherever he goes. After Daddy saw the surgeon, I heard him say, "Spot, I never thought that you'd outlast me, and you old as the hills. But then again you're just a dog and all you ever had to worry about was a feed and a good hunt."

The house is very quite these days, and everyone talks in whispers. Teresa does nearly all the cooking and the rest of us help out with the washing, and keeping a good fire going. All of us hate the scrubbing board and our hands get all sore from the washing soda.

Mammy goes around as though half asleep. She never smiles anymore except when Tom shows up. His wife Nanny waits for him at the crossroads. Daddy doesn't want her in the house or the forge. We don't say the Rosary as much as we used to, and Mammy doesn't check to see if we do our homework. I think that's great and I do very little of it.

Dolly left Colonel Winters and is now working in Dublin. She's going with a fellow from County Longford named Danny Smyth, and she wants to marry him. She asked Daddy about it and he told her to go ahead and not to wait for him to get better. I heard him telling Mammy, "That fellow has a drink problem, and no good will come of it. But what can you do?"

About a week later, the ambulance pulls up at the gate. It's dark and cold outside. Tom and Mammy help Daddy down from the room. Margaret comes home from the convent in Ballymahon to see Daddy before he leaves for Dublin. They stop at the table by the window. I can barely see his face in the light of the paraffin oil lamp. Everyone shakes hands with him, and tells him goodbye. Joe offers him his hand and Daddy tells him, "I want no more to do with you." Joe runs out the door.

Daddy says to Watt, "Look out for your mother and the young ones."

Watt says, " I sure will. You know you don't have to ask." Daddy looks at me and I think he gives me a smile. They go out the door and the three of them walk very slowly toward the ambulance—two people with a small, frail old man between them wearing a black topcoat draped over his shoulders. When he reaches the ambulance, Watt and Mammy help him climb inside the back. This is the last time we ever see our father. I am ten years and ten months old on this cold February evening in 1949.

Dolly goes to see Daddy every day in the Richmond Hospital in Dublin. She works as a housekeeper and the woman of the house tells her to take all the time she needs. She telegraphs the post office in Moyvore most days with any bit of news she can give. Meanwhile, we're back to saying the Rosary at night and the priest is asked to say Masses for a speedy recovery.

A week from the day he left, a car pulls up at the gate with the bad news. Frank, Eddie and I are in bed when Anne comes up and tells us Daddy is dead and we won't have anyone to beat us anymore. Little did she know! When Watt gave his word to take care of us, he took it for granted that it included beating us.

The evening funeral or removal to the church is one of the largest ever seen in Moyvore, according to Tom. As the hearse gets to Moyvore, Spot lies in the middle of the crossroads and the driver has to get out and move him. Those of us who are left at home to keep the house, pull the curtains and say a silent prayer for the passing soul.

Tom tells us that he talked to Father Daly afterwards, who'd come from another parish to be at the funeral, and that Father Daly assured him that Daddy was in heaven and there was no need to cry for him.

Next morning, I'm on my way to school when Margaret stops me at the gate. She says, "You don't go to school on the day of your father's funeral." I don't know this because no one told me. The house is crowded and no one seems to know whether they're coming or going. At least we have some turf in the shed and I don't have to go down the field for sticks.

Maureen arrived home from England and herself, Margaret, Mammy and Dolly are crying most of the time at the house. It's the same in the graveyard.

Standing near the grave as the coffin is lowered, I don't really know how I feel. I have so many feelings going through me that I don't know which is real and which isn't. I look at Mammy, and Tom and Margaret are trying to hold her up, and I wonder, will she fall in the grave if they let go of her?

It's pelting rain and little rivulets of water run down the fresh mound of earth. A lot of the earth has washed away and stones are poking out. I lean over to look in the grave and see there's water in it. The priest's black and white robes blow in the wind and rain. He tosses in three handfuls of wet clay and they make a hollow thud on the coffin. He recites, " Father, Son, and Holy Ghost, and ashes to ashes dust to dust."

The noise of the first shovel of clay hitting the coffin brings me back to reality. This is real, this is cold, this is miserable, this is ugly, this is dread, this is fear, this is death. It's final. I can't cry because I have no tears. I just don't know how to cry. It will take me many years to learn.

Spot goes missing for a few days after that, and Seán finds him in the graveyard lying beside Daddy's grave. He brings Spot home and locks him in the shed.

For want of a nail the shoe was lost.
For want of a shoe the horse was lost.
For want of the horse the rider was lost.
For want of the rider the battle was lost.
For want of the battle the Kingdom was lost.
And all, for want of a nail.

Moaning

Mammy lies in her bed, moaning. She's been in bed since Daddy died, except for one trip to a special doctor in Mullingar. He told her he might have to send her to the Richmond Hospital in Dublin for tests. She says she doesn't want to go there, "Because that's where they took your father and he died."

"You must not have been praying for me, Paidin," she says to me.

I want to tell her, "Yes, I've been praying for you every day and I prayed for Daddy to die when he beat me with the leather belt, and he did die. I know it's is a mortal sin to pray for someone to die and now I'll go to hell and burn forever. I know when I pray for you that God won't listen to me anymore and now you'll die because of me."

The priest came to see her yesterday. He comes in to see her about once a week. If there's no sign of him, Mammy sends one of us to get him.

Teresa puts a white lace cloth over the chair beside the bed, along with a candle, the holy water, and Crucifix. Mammy puts money on it for the priest.

Teresa says, "Isn't that just lovely, there isn't a bite to eat in the house and here you are giving money to the priest."

Mammy says, "Watch your mouth and don't talk like that about the holy man."

119

Teresa says, "Holy, my eye. He came here a short while ago riding a bicycle and now he's driving a new car. Maybe we should all be priests."

Anne pipes in, "Not only a new car, but walks into a farm of land and a house bigger than the chapel."

Mammy turns away from them in the bed and declares she won't listen to their sinful talk.

Margaret has gone back to school in Ballymahon, but Maureen and Carmel—her two-year-old daughter—are still with us. Before Maureen goes back to England she tells Mammy, "Those young children should be taken away by the social services and put in homes where they'll be fed proper food and looked after."

I'm almost eleven and a half and I hope she's just talking about Frank and Eddie. I'll be glad when Maureen goes back, because she's a fussy auld rip and thinks everyone under twelve should be in bed by seven o'clock. When Anne or Teresa give her a cup of tea, she examines the cup all around to see if there's a speck of dirt on it. Anne calls her "sooty wallops" because of her jet-black hair. Maureen gave her a beating for it once, or as she said herself, "a right good hiding." They bring home some strange type of talk from England with them. Maybe that's why Daddy said he'd never see a son of his go to that heathen country where the Angelus bell never rings.

The priest comes and gives Mammy Holy Communion and leaves with the money. He told her to have us boil some nettles and drink the juice twice a day. Now we're out cutting nettles every day and getting stung. It wouldn't be so bad if we had gloves, but all we have are pieces of old rags to save our hands.

I'm the best at getting nettles and I get stuck with the job more than any of them. If push comes to shove, I would rather get stung by a bee or a wasp than a nettle. A bee sting hurts more, but doesn't last as long as a nettle. Sometimes a nettle sting lasts a couple of days. I scratch them real hard and rub paraffin oil on them. That sort of numbs them and they don't pain as much.

Dumplings

It's morning, and we're hungry and cold. We have little food in the house. The fire wasn't raked last night and now we have no hot coals to start it for the day. The last one up at night is supposed to take the ashes from the pit and cover the fire with it. This keeps the fire smoldering till morning. Now, we will have to try and light it with pieces of burning paper.

Seán has caught two blackbirds. He put a small piece of a stick under the edge of the upturned metal oven, tied a string to the stick, and then he brought the string inside the window. He put some dough he made from flour under the oven and when the birds went in to eat, he pulled the stick away and the oven fell down—trapping the birds.

Teresa and Anne try to make dumplings, but the buttermilk is old and it looks like white liver floating on white water. They put the dumplings in the saucepan with the blackbirds and boil them. The saucepan is too small and everything sticks together and has to be removed all at once. The dumplings are soft on the outside and like putty on the inside and taste like shite, but we eat them anyway. Later, we have some fun making up a verse:

Oh those dumplings,
those terrible dumplings.
They were made from flour,
buttermilk, some salt and soda.
And they were drowned,
in blackbird soup.

Most of the summer goes by and Mammy stays in bed. Doctor Joyce comes and tells her she won't have to go to Dublin after all, as he has cured her himself. She seems to pick up a little bit with that news. He calls Teresa and Anne aside and tells them, "Get your mother up every day and take her for a walk or she'll never get out of that bed."

They do this for about a week and she starts getting up on her own, but she still goes around as if in a daze.

Something I Ate

The weather gets better and we can hear the crackle of the horses and carts going to the bog. Anne and I are still tasked with bringing the water from the village pump. On our way back with the water, we see the men playing skittles at the crossroads. Skittles are round pieces of wood about eight inches long and nearly two inches thick. They stand them in rows of four, three, two and one at the front. They roll another stick along the road to try and knock the pieces down from about twenty-five feet. Each person gets two chances to knock the ten skittles. I want to play too.

Anne complains to Mammy, "Paidin gets lazier by the new time and I have to stop several times on the way home so he can rest with one simple bucket of water."

They all keep calling me lazy bones, but I don't care what they say. They can all go and suck a fish's tit for all I care. And what's more, they can go and cut the nettles themselves from now on. I'm going to clamp turf for Christy Mahon, Peggy's brother. He came in and asked Mammy after Mass this morning. He wanted Chris, but Chris is busy with Tom Cormack. I got a big thorn in my shoulder when I fell on the bundle of sticks I was carrying and it festered and is sore as hell. Between that and feeling tired and sleepy, I want to rest a lot of the time. I go to bed early to be rested for the morning's work with Christy Mahon, but I can't sleep for thinking of the bog and not having to go to school. But still what is a little sleep to a person when there are two week's work ahead on the bog?

I get up early the next morning and take the long way around the crossroads to Puttingham. I could cut across Bob Mearse's field, but he keeps a young bull in the field. Chris told me the bull chased him last week and nearly got him. He claims he barely made it through the

fence on time. I'm dead tired by the time I get to Peggy Mahon's—
tired like when I had the measles, only I don't have any red spots.
Peggy offers me tea and bread and I tell her no thanks. I go outside to
the paddock to bridle the mare, and when I lead her back, I see Peggy
and Christy whispering to each other.

Myself and Christy get the mare yoked to the cart and then
Christy says to me, "You're going home, young fellow." I don't
understand. He takes me home and tells Mammy, "That young lad is
sick, Mrs. Burke. You should take him to the doctor."

I go to bed and fall asleep. It seems like only a few minutes later
when Teresa is waking me. She wants me to go into the box room
because the doctor is coming to see me and she doesn't want him
going in the room with that broken down bed and dirty blankets. She
tells me I've been asleep for over three hours.

I get up and go to the kitchen because I don't want the doctor
seeing me in bed, in case he might think I'm sick, but they won't let
me stay up and I don't feel like fighting them.

The doctor comes and he still has those red-rimmed glasses I
remember from when I was younger. He sticks a pair of rubbery
looking things in his ears and puts the round shiny end on my chest
and then on my back. He must have had the thing out all night
because it's freezing cold. Then he puts his hand flat on my chest and
taps it with his fingers. He takes a little flashlight from his bag and
shines it into my eyes. I think I must have very dark eyes that he needs
a flashlight to look in them.

He leaves the room and I overhear him saying to Mammy, "I'll
send the ambulance out in the morning. Now don't worry, they will
probably just keep him a few days."

I don't like the idea of the ambulance coming for me. I keep
seeing Daddy's face when it came for him. It brought him away, but
it didn't bring him back again. Then it strikes me all of a sudden. This
is God's way of punishing me for my sins. All my cursing and
fighting, stealing and telling lies, pissing in Mrs. O' Kelly's kettle
and letting her make the tea with it and her and the priest drinking it.
Then I think of hiding down the fields like Seán did, but I know I

can't because I don't feel strong enough, and besides if I hide in Seán's old hide-out they'll find me in no time flat.

I decided there's nothing for it but to go in the ambulance, and let God take me if he wants. I bet auld Nick is already stoking the fire for me, and he won't have to rake it like we do. It's probably a thousand times bigger and burns all night. Or maybe I'll feel better in the morning and I won't have to go at all. Wouldn't that shake them. As soon as Doctor Joyce leaves, Anne tells me to get out of her bed, and says, "You better not have peed in it." She doesn't sound as mean as usual. I wonder, does she know I'm going to die like Daddy?

I sneak into the back room and look for my britches, but there's not a sign of them, or my shirt. I shout for Anne, asking if she saw my britches and she tells me it's drying at the fire with my shirt. That does it! That pair of witches washed my clothes and now I have no choice but to stay in bed. Maybe I should put them on my list like Mrs.O'Kelly.

Their bed in the box room is nice and soft and doesn't have boards across it holding up the mattress. I suppose the girls didn't jump up and down on the beds like the lads did in the back room. I keep thinking about tomorrow and what will happen. Maybe I should pray, but what good will that do? God doesn't listen to bad people except in confession, and that isn't until Friday. Of course I could say an act of contrition and wouldn't that keep me safe until then? That's it. I start saying acts of contrition all evening and I say at least fifty before I fall asleep.

The ambulance comes at ten o clock and Mammy, Teresa and Anne walk me out to it. We go to the back door where Daddy got in, and the driver says, "No, that young man is getting in the front with me." This gives me a little hope. Maybe the ones who aren't going to die get to ride up front.

The three of them are talking and I hear Mammy say, "Paidin, you'll be home again in a few days." I'm just glad they aren't shaking my hand and saying goodbye like they did with Daddy.

I climb into the front seat, and just as the driver starts to close the door, Anne leans inside and kisses me on my cheek. God, I could kill her! What in hell's tarnation does she think she's doing? You don't go around kissing people on the jaw in front of everyone—especially with the driver watching. It's the first time this has ever happened to me, and I've never seen it happen to anyone else. I'm ready to kill her and I wonder what the driver must think. I have to get out of that hospital now, if only to let Anne have it! I keep glancing at him on the way to Mullingar and he seems to be a nice man.

When we arrive at the hospital, he shows me to the desk and I hand the note from the doctor to the woman in white. She speaks to another woman who tells me to follow her. We walk down a wide hallway leading to a large ward with lots of beds. She brings me to a bed and tells me to climb in, and that she'll be back in a few minutes.

After what seems like forever, she comes back with a doctor who examines me the same way Doctor Joyce did. He takes the sheet of paper clipped to the end of the bed on a board, writes on it, and gives some instructions to the nurse that I don't understand. They both leave without a word and she comes back with a small tray with a thin rubber hose and a syringe like the dentist had in school. She ties the rubber hose around my arm above the elbow, and then sticks the needle in my arm and fills up the syringe with my blood.

"There now," she says. "Surely that didn't hurt." I wonder—how does she know when it wasn't stuck in her? A few days later she does the same thing, except this time she puts blood in me instead of taking it out. The needle is taped to my arm and a thin hose runs into a bottle of blood hanging over the head of the bed. In a few days I begin feeling better and I want to get up, but they won't let me. During the next week, I have several pints of blood to go with the pills they keep giving me.

Two old men on either side of me can't eat anything hard like apples, because they have no teeth, so they give their apples to me. My stay in the hospital lasts six weeks and during this time six people die in that ward. The first time I see the screen around a bed I sneak over and peek in. It's my first sight of a dead person and it sends the shivers up my back. I can't wait to get home to start climbing trees, going for a hunt, or even kicking stones.

125

Just about when I think I'm in for life, the nurse comes and tells me, "Pat, you're going home today."

I jump so high I nearly bite my tongue when I land. The journey home seems to take forever. The ambulance finally lets me out at the gate and when I go in they're so happy to see me you'd think I'd just come home from America. Anne is making toast with the tongs; she has the slice of bread sitting on the legs of the tongs and holding it over the fire. She brings it over to the table and butters it. Then she does something that really confuses me; she hands the slice of toast to me.

"There," she says. "Paidin, that will help you get better, but don't expect it too often." I've never known her to do that before, and I wonder if she's sick.

I ask Mammy what malnutrition means. She looks at me and says, "Why do you ask that?"

When I tell her that one doctor said something about it to the nurse when I first went in, she says, "It must be something you ate."

Teresa looks at her with the whites of her eyes and says, "You mean something he didn't eat."

I decide then and there not to say anything about neglect in case that's also something I ate. I gobble down the tea and toast and leave them to their chat while Spot and I head off down the fields, hoping for a hunt.

Chapter Nine

A Robbery

Shaw's pub and grocery was broken into and robbed during the small hours of the morning. The thieves used an auger to bore holes in the front door beside the lock and bolt, and then opened the door. They took all they could carry with them, including all the books and ledgers and cigarettes. Watt wasn't too happy when he heard about it because he'd just paid off our big bill for the funeral and wiped the slate clean.

Mammy asked him if he got a receipt for it and he said he didn't think to, as we've have been dealing with John McQuaid for donkey's years and it was never a problem. He was more upset about the cigarettes being stolen than anything else. He said he hoped his were kept upstairs in storage—if not, then John Mc Quaid would answer to him for it. Watt has gotten real contrary and bossy since Daddy died, especially after he had to sell the cow to pay the bills. Now he thinks he can beat us the same as Daddy did. It doesn't work with me and he gets real mad when I won't do what he tells me. He gave me a fierce beating last week and I still defied him.

When he hit Chris and Anne for the umpteenth time that did it. Mammy told him, "No more! That's it. You don't hit any of them again in this house, and if you do, you can pack your bags."

He cleared off and went to Coventry where Joe got him a job, and we were all glad to see the end of him.

Detectives came out from Mullingar and asked the McQuaids all sorts of questions, like how come they never heard anything and they being just upstairs. A short while after that, John McQuaid and his family left for parts unknown. A new manager took over for a few months, and then it was sold to a Liam McAuley from Roscommon. He's a good-looking fellow, well dressed, and sings in the choir and plays football.

Mammy applied for and got a widow's non-contributory pension. They told her in Mullingar it's based on the needs of her family, and that she would do all right seeing as she had six children under the age of eighteen. She says, "Sure maybe between that and the children's allowance money we can survive. But then, sure isn't it little enough."

Anne puts an arm around her and says, "Sure Modleen, won't you find a man and get married again? And this time make sure you find a rich one to keep us all living in comfort."

"Yes," Mammy says, "and maybe have another bauld daughter like you to pester me. Then I'd be made for life! Get out of here you little hussy, before I leather you." She gets up from her chair and goes to the room. When the door closes, we hear the sucking in of her breath as she inhales her snuff.

Rosie Crinegan got her started on it some time back, telling Mammy it would help to settle her nerves. She really took to the snuff, and now the area around her nose and mouth is all brown from it, along with the rag she stuffs in the little pocket of her apron. She thinks no one will know if she goes and does it in the room, but we all know, and this only brings more attention to it. Teresa and Anne both agree it's a fierce dirty habit. They hate the way she puts it on the back of her hand and sucks it up one side and then the other. Still, they warn me not to say anything about it to her or anyone.

"Why not?" I ask, and they tell me it helps to keep her mind off Daddy and she gets pleasure out of it.

"Be Janey," Anne says, "that's what we should all do, use snuff. Just look, can't you just imagine Paidin using snuff. Wouldn't he look just great with those pair of candles hanging out of him, especially if they were part brown to go with the green and white. Why who knows, we might even put some Christmas decorations on him and he'd do as a Christmas tree?"

I tell her, "At least I'd be good for something, not like you, you long-legged, going-into-the-middle-of-next-week bitch."

She can sure get me vexed; sometimes I could hit her a good one.

The nuns came and asked Mammy if there was any way at all they could keep Margaret as a boarder for her last year. They said she was such a good pupil it would be a shame if she didn't finish. Mammy said there was no way she could come up with the money. Then Margaret got a bike and encouraged Anne to go along with her, so they ride to school together each day.

I feel sorry for Teresa because she has to do all the cooking and washing. Mammy doesn't do much, but at least she gets up every day and isn't in the bed moaning anymore. Teresa says she has to try and make a meal from nothing. Mostly that means potatoes and white sauce made from milk flour and onions, with butter when we have it. The cry she usually hears from us when we get home from school is, "Teresa, did you make the sauce?"

Chris, who's going to the technical school in Ballymahon, calls her "the white sauce Queen of Moyvore." She doesn't like that and threatens to let him go hungry.

I'm getting in my usual trouble at school, mostly for not doing my homework. Most days start for me with a couple of slaps, except when I came home from the hospital, Mrs. O'Kelly didn't hit me for a few days. I try to get my own back at Mrs O'Kelly by hook or crook. Last week when I made the fire, I put six chestnuts in it. She was sitting in her usual way with one leg on each side of it when it blew up her skirt with a fierce bang. She jumped up screaming and trying to get the hot cinders off her thighs. Her face turned as white as her hair, and she had to go home for two hours while the infants' teacher watched the two classrooms. When she got back, several of the girls were only too glad to tell her I'd put chestnuts in the fire. She sure didn't spare the stick on me, and forbade me to make the fire again.

Next day, when I went to the lavatory, I got the frog I'd hidden in a jar and went to the girls' cloakroom and put it in the pocket of her topcoat. She blamed Joe Cormack for it and I said nothing. But I heard she did a bit of squealing when she put her hand in her pocket.

Joe is a mad devil and always up to something. We call him Red Joe. He has only five weeks to go till he's fourteen, and he says the minute he turns fourteen, that will be all she'll see of him. No more school for him, and no Mrs. O'Kelly. "No, no never again," says Joe. I have nearly a year and a half to go, if I last that long. All of us boys have one thing in common with Joe—we hate Mrs. O'Kelly.

I didn't know it until later, but the ambulance driver who took me to the hospital was Joe's father. They live up in Doneel and he seldom comes in to Moyvore. He gets all their messages and shopping in Mullingar. Joe says he's not a bad auld fart when you get to know him. I don't think I would ever have got to know my father like that, not if he'd lived to be a hundred—and if I had called him a name like that, it would be the last thing I ever did.

Joe went out to the lavatory and stood in the hallway with Mrs. O Kelly's hat on his head. We could see him through the glass door putting on faces like a clown. The priest came on him of a sudden and he had to stick the hat under his coat. He had the hat in the classroom and didn't know what to do with it. He kept asking to go to the lavatory so he could leave it back in the cloakroom, and she kept saying no. Meantime the big blue feather in it broke. The priest left and Mrs. O Kelly told Bridie Early to go for her coat and hat. Joe was in a panic and again asked to go to the lavatory.

She said, "Okay then, if you're so desperate."

He caught Bridie in the hall before she came in and handed her the hat with a warning not to say a thing about it under pain of death. Bridie got a slap for being such a numbscull and breaking the feather.

Miss Finnerty, the teacher for the infants' class, bought a new Ford prefect car. She parks it out front by the wall where Mrs. O' Kelly leaves her bike. Joe tied the wheel of the bike to the mudguard of the car underneath with a rope, and then hid the rope with grass. When Miss Finnerty drove away that evening the bike went with her and she didn't notice it till she was near the crossroads.

A Wedding

Dolly got married to Danny Smyth today and Chris served the Mass for the wedding. Danny gave him six shillings, the most anyone ever got in Moyvore for serving at a wedding. I wonder how much the priest got.

I served Mass at Pat Leavy's wedding and got nothing but a thank you. He married Agnes Rodgers who already had a kid and she single, the same as her sister, Kathleen. The two children were rattling the iron gate when Red Gaffney was driving his cattle past their house one day, and the cattle ran off on him. He hit the gate beside them with his ash plant and called them a pair of little bastards. Red is a rich man according to what Seán Rodgers says and so mean and stingy he still has his christening money.

Red's sister Eileen walks to Moyvore twice a week for the shopping. She's a blond-haired girl who's always smiling. If anyone speaks to her, she answers hallo with a big smile. Mammy says the poor thing is innocent, and not all there. Mrs. Crinegan says she has bats in the belfry, and all those Gaffneys are a bit odd. Her brother, Red, was always beating her up till Father Tom went down to him about it. He told him if he ever raised a hand to her again, he would put elephant's ears on him. Mammy said he could do it too, because that man has great powers.

Rosie Crinegan said, "He might have, and he might not. Father Mc Manus, when he was here, had more power than him."

Anyway the beating stopped, but Eileen was taken away shortly after that to some kind of a home. And people said Red was doing more than beating her. I don't know what else he could be doing, except maybe starving her. There's a window in the gable end of Joe Rodgers's house and Pat Leavy would use a ladder to climb in late at night to visit Agnes. He'd leave early in the morning before anyone got up.

One morning, Joe Rodgers was waiting for him, and just when he got out on the ladder, he pulled it and Pat fell and hurt his arm real bad. Joe said later, "That put a stop to late night visits at my house."

When he was getting married, the priest asked, " Do you, Patrick Leavy, take Agnes Rodgers for your lawful wedded wife?"

"Indeed I do, Father, sure you know well I do."

"Just say, I do."

"I do, Father."

I thought Father O'Connell seemed awful cross. "And do you, Agnes Rodgers, take Patrick Leavy for your lawful wedded husband?"

"I do, Father."

"I now pronounce you man and wife."

He didn't say the usual, "Go in peace." Like he did today for Dolly and Danny.

Our house is full of people and we've lots of lemonade, cake, sweets, and whiskey and Guinness. The women have two bottles of Sandyman port wine. It's all laid out with the wedding cake on the big table that even has a tablecloth on it. Dolly and Danny cut the cake with the bread knife and pieces of the hard white icing fly all over the place. I wonder why the two of them have to cut it at the same time.

Anne tells me it's a tradition, I don't know what that is either. I do know the cake tastes as good as sweets, even if it is as hard as a bullet and can knock lumps out of your teeth. I hope that means the grown people can't eat it, and it will be all for us children. But it doesn't happen that way, because after everyone has a piece of it Dolly wraps it up to take back to Dublin.

Everyone is in a good mood and even Mammy smiles for the first time in a long while. Mrs. Keegan gave her a glass of port wine and Teresa says it's doing wonders for her. Seán Rodgers plays some tunes on the mouth organ and sings the "Rose of Aranmore." Teresa sings her usual, "If I were a blackbird, I'd whistle and sing and I would follow the ship that my true love sailed in." When she finishes, Anne asks her, "How could you be a blackbird and you a thrush?" Then she says, "Wait till this is all over and I tell Mammy how you got drunk on port wine."

Teresa laughs and tells her, "I don't give a damn what you tell her, and maybe you aught to have a drop yourself; it might take the twist out of your knickers."

Anne says, "I might at that."

Tom is calling for quiet because he wants to sing. Mammy tells him it's polite to wait till you're asked. He rubs her head and says, "Not at all, woman, sure, a man is entitled to sing at his sister's wedding." He starts off with his favorite song "The Bard of Armagh."

Seán Rodgers says, "Well good on you, Tom Burke, now you're clocking ninety, or as they say in Mullingar that's your mowl."

Tom finishes and seems happy with the big clap he gets.

Paheen O'Hearn is asked for a song and says he hasn't brought his singing voice along, but will dance a jig if Seán Rodgers would be kind enough to play for him. He's a half brother of Mrs. Keegan and the only half brother in Moyvore. There are no half sisters either. I don't know how God makes half brothers, but I do know he wasn't found under a head of cabbage like Mammy said Eddie was. Some people call him Andy Round Legs because his knees and his toes turn in as though he was riding a horse. Mary Dinegan, the tinker, was camped on the Chapel Road and asked him for a piece of tobacco for her pipe. It was raining heavy, so he got into her tent, where they both enjoyed a smoke. Then someone heard about it and made up a little song:

You all know Andy Round Legs that smokes the fancy pipe.

He smoked with Mary Dinegan lying in her camp.

When Mary looked at Andy, his face was full of joy.

She said are you the round-legged skalpeen that comes from Ochnaboy.

Someone called him Andy Round Legs in Egan's pub and he got so vexed he slashed the back of that person's hand with his penknife. He lives in through the fields behind Rodger's house in Ochnaboy. He's a very nervous man and one time when he got lost in the dark going home, he went through the fields shouting, "Help! Man astray! Man astray!"

People tease him a lot and Mammy says it's not right. Someone put a sheet on their head one dark night and stood in the ditch, and when Paheen saw it, he ran all the way to Moyvore, shouting that he'd seen the Banshee. If you see the Banshee it means you or someone close to you is going to die.

Seán starts to play and Paheen breaks into his dance. Pat Shanley lets out a cheer and tells him, "Now you're thrashing with the belt off." He dances real good for a while, and then he stops, bent over with his hands on his knees and a dribble coming from his mouth. He's sucking in air like the flapper on the forge bellows. He says he's not as young as he used to be. He gets a big clap and stands straight up proud as a turkey cock.

Order is called for, and then Mammy is asked to give a recitation. She doesn't have to be asked twice. Mrs. Keegan asks her to give the one about the young man in the church. Mammy says, "You mean the poor scholar?" She explains how this young man went into a protestant church by mistake. He thought it was a Catholic church and he said:

At the church door I entered I stood in the center.
I gazed with admiration.
I viewed each pew along my view and how they were situated.
I forgot my place till I blessed my face with the sign of the Crucifixion.
You'd think I insulted the man on the pulpit,
For without any hesitation, he asked me my name and from hence I came and what was my occupation.
"Indeed, kind sir," said the lad, "It is with your leave
as you do crave, I'm of this Irish nation.
And I'm of the Papish breed, which I can read my seed, breed, and generation.
And I came to be here without dread or fear of your grand exaltation."
"Well, indeed my noble youth," said the minister.
"If you wish to know the truth, and how to shun perdition, you

would renounce your Pope with that on oath and all his superstition.
You would not care for saints or prayers, images, or imitations.
The Blessed Virgin you would not invoke; she is but a joke and cannot hear your petition.
But your Priest and I are like two of a trade; we'd wish for each other's destruction."

"Then, my God," I said, "It sets me mad and puts me in confusion, to think our church is bad that was blessed by God and built on a rock's foundation.

It reigned for sixteen hundred years without dread or fear or the least molestation.

Till Luther the Fryer came to make God's scripture a liar and then began the Reformation.

'Twas to England he came in King Henry's reign where he got reformation and married Ann Boleyn which he was sorry for—and that by his own confession.

How can this Church stand when it is built on sand and water running beneath the foundation?

But it was King Henry laid the first stone of this grand exaltation and forever more it will be slithering down to damnation."

Pat Shanley says, "Missus, that's a grand poem, I never heard that one before. Where did you get it?"

Mammy says, "I got it from my grandfather and he got it from his. It's been in our family for years."

Pat tells her, "It sure is a great one, and tells a real story. Would you ever write it out for me when you get a chance?"

Mammy says, "I certainly will." She seems real happy to be the center of attention. Margaret calls for order that she might recite a poem. She says she learned this poem about a village blacksmith by Longfellow, and she'd like to recite it especially for Mammy. She starts:

Under a spreading chestnut-tree
The village smithy stands:

The smith, a mighty man is he,
With large and sinewy hands:
And the muscles of his brawny arms
are strong as iron bands.
His hair is crisp, and black and long,
his face is like the tan:
his brow is wet with honest sweat,
he earns whate'er he can,
and looks the whole world in the face
for he owes not any man.
Week in, week out, from morn till night,
you can hear his bellows blow:
You can hear him swing his heavy sledge,
with measured beat and slow,
like a sexton ringing the village bell,
when the evening sun is low.
And children coming home from school
look in at the open door:
They love to hear the flaming forge,
and bear the bellows roar,
and catch the burning sparks that fly
like chaff from a threshing-floor.

He goes on Sunday to the church,
and sits among his boys:
He hears the parson pray and preach,
he hears his daughters voice,
singing in the village choir,
and it makes his heart rejoice.
It sounds to him like her mother's voice.
singing in paradise!
He needs must think of her once more,
how in the grave she lies:
and with his haul, rough hand he wipes
a tear out of his eyes.

Toilin-rejoicing- sorrowing,
onward through life he goes;
each morning sees some task begin,
each evening sees it close.
Something attempted, something done,
has earned a night's repose.
Thanks, thanks to thee, my worthy friend,
for the lesson thou hast taught!
Thus at the flaming forge of light
our fortunes must be wrought.
Thus on its sounding anvil shaped
each burning deed and thought.

"Now tell me, Margaret," says Pat Shanley, "would that Longfellow be Eamon De Valera, because they call him the Longfellow."

"No, Pat," says Margaret. "It's Henry Wadsworth Longfellow, an American writer and poet." Mammy has started to cry and Margaret puts her arm around her.

"Are you alright, Mammy?" Margaret asks.

Teresa tells her, "You aught to know better than recite a poem about a blacksmith. Now look what you've done! She'll be crying now for God knows how long."

Mammy uses her handkerchief to wipe her tears. Then she mutters, "Oh, I'm okay. I was just thinking of your daddy."

The celebration goes on till late evening and then the men go to the pub while we all pitch in to clean up. Next morning all is back to normal and Dolly and Danny head back for Dublin.

Election Day

It's general Election Day and Mammy has put the kettle on to make tea for Mrs. Crinegan, who's looking out the window. She sees

Rosie Crinegan coming and says, "Take off the kettle, Mrs. Burke. Here comes Rosie." The two women have the same name, they aren't related. The only thing they have in common is a real dislike for each other.

Rosie is a short little woman with a goiter. She has a wizened face, and looks a bit like James Finn (the fellow who Chris said looks like Gabby Hayes). She lives in a two-story cottage in Pearsetown about two and a half miles from Moyvore, but she walks to Moyvore twice a week with a straw shopping bag to get groceries. She says she likes to get fresh bread twice a week. Everyone knows she does it to get tobacco for her pipe. One time in our house she was rooting in her bag for her snuffbox, and her tobacco fell out. She told Mammy it was for a neighbor. Mammy remarked later, "As though I didn't know she smokes."

Rosie sits at the fire warming her hands and says to no one in particular. "Isn't it fierce cold for the time of year that's in it?"

Mrs. Crinegan says, "It sure is, and worse still the wireless says there's a deep impression over the Alantic, and troughs with no pressure."

Mammy tries to keep a straight face. "So you do have a wireless, Mrs. Crinegan?" asks Rosie.

"Well, I'll have you know, my dear Rosie woman, that I had a wireless long before you ever heard of one. And what's more, it's paid for and not on the never never like some I could mention."

Rosie says, "That may be so, that may be so, but having it paid for won't make it play any better."

"Tell me who did you vote for, Rosie?"

"Well, who do you think I voted for? I voted for DeValera."

"Feck Dev," says Mrs. Crinegan, "what did Dev ever do for me and I a poor widow woman?"

Rosie says, "He gave me a shilling raise in the pension and I know he did as much for you as he did for me, up Dev."

Mammy drops the tea leaves in the big aluminum tea pot from her fingers. She never uses a spoon for this. I wonder how she gets the right amount that way. She does a lot of things in threes. Three times in the tea canister and three times in the pot. Trinity, Cross, and three leaf Shamrock. Rosie asks Mammy if she voted. Mammy says she voted early this morning.

"Sure you'd be voting for Dev. Wasn't Joe Burke always a strong Fianna Fáil and Dev man?"

Mammy says, "He was, but one time he was tempted to vote Fine Gael. Then he said he wouldn't bother because they were all alike and good for nothing."

Rosie says, "They're thinking of raising the children's allowance to a half crown, and that will be good for you, Mrs. Burke, another thing we can thank Dev for." She starts singing the going song about it.

The other night De Valera he said in the Dail.
The population of Ireland these late years did fall.
And to increase it and not let it down,
To every child born he gave a half crown
I'm a young single man and I'm tired of life.
I said I'd go out in search of a wife.
I married a widow and then settled down,
To try to rare children to get this half crown.
Now this job has proved harder than people may think,
For since I got married I've slept ne'er a wink.
My wife she keeps at me and calls me a clown,
And says I do nothing to get this half crown.

Mrs. Crinegan gives her a dirty look. Mammy hands them the tea, butter, and bread she baked this morning.

Mrs. Early walks in with a big hello for everybody. She's a tall, dark-haired woman with glasses who lives near Rosie in Pearsetown. She tells people's fortunes by reading the tea leaves in the cups. Mammy is a bit leery of her since the time she told Mammy we were going to lose livestock. That night Watt's ferret got out of the barrel where he kept him and killed four of Mammy's six hens. Our house ate well that week and so did Tom's. We found the barrel lying on its side next morning. Watt said the ferret sure as hell didn't knock it over, and he would bet anything she had her sons do it. Mammy told Watt he'd have to get rid of that ferret. But he didn't have to.

That same day he put the ferret in to a rat's hole where they fought and squealed for twenty minutes. When he dug them out, the ferret still had a hold of the dead rat. The ferret died a week later, and Watt said the rat poisoned him. That was several months ago—the end of Watt's ferret, and the end of rabbit stew.

Mammy hands Mrs. Early the tea and bread, and gets her own. The four of them sit around the fire on the four chairs. That leaves only the stool and one leg of that is always falling out. I hope they don't have two cups of tea, because there isn't much milk left. Teresa beckons Anne and myself to come outside, where Anne says, "All we need now is Mae Rodgers for the stool." Although she says Mae is a decent sort.

Teresa says, "That's right, but those other two are auld biddy's. They've been coming here for years with one arm as long as the other. They never even bring a biscuit in the house. Now just you wait and see. There won't be a drop of milk in the house this evening, and Mammy is worse to be giving it to them."

Anne says Mrs. Crinegan has a small farm and a pension and neither chick nor child to care for.

Mammy calls me to bring in some turf for the fire. I bring in an armful and they pull back the chairs so I can put it on the fire. That done, they close in again to continue their chat. Rosie asks Mammy, "How do you spell voucher?"

Mammy spells it for her and Mrs. Crinegan asks Rosie if she's going to apply for the free boots. Rosie says, "I am and I amn't. And even if I am it's my affair and no one else's."

The only time the word voucher was heard in Moyvore was in regard to the free boots. Teresa says the only reason they hate each other is that they both want to be on the right side of Mammy. After all Burke's is a great place to get the tea on their way to and from the village.

When she sees they're leaving, Teresa asks me to dig some potatoes from the garden. She says she'll make some nice white sauce if they left any milk. I find a few of the potatoes Chris and I sowed last year, with the stocks all withered from the winter. I don't know if the spade is behind them or on top of them when I dig. I get a good half-bucket, wash them at the barrel of water, and head for the warmth of the house.

Chapter Ten

Dead Ass

Nan Scally died in the Mullingar Hospital. She was in there just a very short time. Most people understood she just had an appendix removed and would be home soon. She was two years older than George, in the same class with my sister Anne. Mae Rodgers brought the news on her way to the village. Then Mrs. Crinegan came in crying and Mammy said, "I know how you feel, Mrs. Crinegan. Isn't it awful about that poor young girl dying at such a young age?"

Mrs. Crinegan blows her nose with her handkerchief and says, "Everyone has their own troubles, Mrs. Burke. My poor ass died last night. When I got up this morning, I found him dead in the haggard and the poor thing died all on his own, with not even a calf to keep him company."

God, I think, here it comes. She's going to blame me for killing him. I borrowed the ass and worked him pretty hard, and now he's dead. I went to Williamstown bog for a load of turf, and then I went for a load of turnips. I'd only borrowed him to get the turf, but when I got home with it, Tom came and asked if I would go and get a load of turnips for him above Jim Finn's. Tom has a pig he's is fattening up to sell. I told him, "No way! I only got the ass for the day and I want to bring at least two loads of turf from the bog." But he said he'd give me two shillings, and that did it. It was all the convincing I needed.

The big clamp of turf is about two hundred yards in off the gravel road, and I had to go in through the wet bog three times to bring out enough to make a good load. I brought out two small jogs and tipped

142

them up at the side of the road. On the way out with the third one, the wheel of the cart went down to the axle. I had to unload all the turf and try to get that stubborn jack ass to pull out the empty cart.

They say a mule is stubborn, but I think an ass is worse. They will only go at their own pace, whether one likes it or not. I got it unloaded and pulled forward just enough that we were on solid footing and I could throw the turf back on. I don't know how long it took, but it seemed forever before I got the cart out of the hole and threw the other two jogs on it. I packed it up over the top of the crates and it made for a fine big load of turf. I wanted to sit up on it for the trip home, but I couldn't because of the potholes in the road. The holes were full of water and I wanted the ass to walk in them so the wheels would be on the good part of the road. If I let the wheels go in those potholes I could break an axle or something and lose a lot of the turf. So I had to take him by the head and lead him into them. This meant I had to walk the mile and a half home. It was about a mile to the main road, and clear sailing from there. But I still couldn't get on top, because it wouldn't look good going up through the village with a big load of turf on the poor ass and me on top. It's not that he couldn't do it because he was a big auld jack ass and as strong as a mule. It just would not look good, especially if Mrs. Crinegan saw me. She can be a mad old biddy, and she swears like a trooper when she gets mad.

I made a deal with her for the ass. I agreed to give her a day's work for every day I had him. We were making the hay in the two-acre field. It was nice and sunny and she decided to let the two calves out for a while, and then a shower came. We tried to get them in, but one was very frisky and the more I ran after him the more he kicked up his heels like a young filly. It took me over a half an hour before I got him back in the shed. By this time she was white with temper and she snapped the hasp on the door and said, "Paidin, you just wait here and I'll take cake care of that Boyo." She went in the house where she keeps a small statue of nearly every Saint known to man, lined up on a big table in the parlor. She prays to them all in turn and if she doesn't get what she prays for, she puts a black cloth over that particular statue and prays to the others. Mammy asked her what would happen if they were all in black, and she said she leaves them in limbo and turns to the Blessed Virgin.

She came out with a black thorn stick and started beating the calf, along with a fit of swearing the likes of which was never heard. "You little bastard, you must think I have nothing better to do than run after you all day, when I'm a busy woman with hay lying in the field." She keeps swearing and hitting, and the poor calf is trembling.

Just as I'm working up the courage to try and stop her, Father Tom comes around the corner. I want to tell her the priest is coming, but it's too late, he's too close and he'd hear me. I don't know which of them I'm more scared of. He comes and looks in the door at her and asks, "Are you talking to yourself, Mrs. Crinegan?"

" No, I am not," she says, "I'm talking to that little bastard."

Father Tom nearly falls back in the evergreen hedge with the laughter. I can't see what he has to laugh about. It doesn't seem very funny seeing a little calf being beaten.

She closes the door and says to Father Tom, "I hope you haven't come here to preach to me, because I'm a busy woman right now."

He looks at me and asks me if I have anything to do. I know by the look on his face that I'd better get out of there in a hurry. I skidaddle off down the field, and start turning the hay. The weather took up for five days after that and we got to save the field of hay.

When I got home with the load of turf, I tipped it up at the shed, then I grabbed some bread and jam, wolfed it down with tea, and hit out for Jim Finn's of Cloncullen to get Tom's turnips.

Cloncullen is about a mile and a half from Moyvore and the day was growing short. I got to Finn's and Jim helped me load the cart from a pit in the field. Jim and Tom were good friends and he spent a lot of time in our house in the old days. Then Dolly went to Dublin and he stopped the visits. They walked out quite a few times together, but she never did admit that there was anything to it. Daddy told Dolly not to see him anymore, as he was too old for her. She was getting out the window one night to go to a dance with him and stepped right into the barrel of water Daddy put there. Her new dress was ruined and Daddy told her, "That's what you get for defying your father."

Mrs. Crinegan was always after Jim, and even told Mammy they were a little more than good friends and she was hoping to be asked a big question one of the days. When Jim heard it, he said he already had a mother and what would he want with another? She heard it back and put a stream of her colorful curses on him, and she said it included all his kith and kin.

Between the Ballymore Road and Dalystown Road there are just two farms, James Keane's and Paul Rooney's. Both farms stretch from the Ballymore Road all the way over to the Dalystown Road. James Keane is the biggest farmer in Moyvore, with over nine hundred acres of land. As I came down the Ballymore Road with my load of turnips, I could see across the fields all the way to Tom's house and the hill of Halston. I thought if there was a road across them fields I'd get there in no time flat. Instead I had to go all the way down to our crossroads, which is about three quarters of a mile, and then take the main road to Baltackin Cross and the Dalystown Road.

I passed Rooney's haggard where we did the threshing last year. The threshing machine belongs to Paddy Mulvaney, who lives down the rock road. I barely remember when I was very small and late one night he was outside our house shouting, "Come out, Burke, and fight like a man."

Mammy told him, "Go home, Paddy Mulvaney, and have a bit of common sense." Then he banged on the door and Tom got up to him. There was a scuffle in the kitchen and Mammy was saying, "No, Tom, you'll kill him." I heard someone say later that Tom had him across the table, choking him.

Paddy does all the threshing for the farmers and Rooney's is usually the first, it being the closest. The thresher has iron wheels, and he pulls it with a blue tractor. It makes enough noise to wake the dead, and can be heard all over the countryside like the Angelus' bell. He pulls it in beside the big reek of wheat in Rooney's haggard. A long belt runs from the flywheel of the tractor to a wheel on the side of the threshing machine. Then wooden blocks are jammed under the wheels of each to stop any movement and keep the belt tight. Two men pitch the sheaves and two boys cut the twine that binds them.

Paddy Mulvaney feeds the wheat into the machine, where big tumblers make a whirring sound as they fly around. The straw comes out one end and is taken away and built in a big reek. The grain comes out the other end in slots that have hooks to hold the sacks as they fill up. Philip Keegan and I cut the belts. We started at nine in the morning and worked till it was almost dark. We had one stop for lunch. By evening my hand was sore and nearly blistered from the knife. Philip Keegan was more tired than I was, and failed to cut a lot of the belts pitched to his side. Near the end of the day I was cutting both his and my own.

I was worried that it would happen, and it did. I was reaching over to cut one of his and he cut the back of my hand. Paddy Mulvaney stopped feeding the machine and told him he was tired and to go take a rest. I finished the last half hour on my own.

I finally got to Tom's house and unloaded the turnips. Nanny gave me tea with bread and jam, and before I left she says, "Tom said he'll see you later." I hoped it wasn't like the last time he promised me a shilling, because he never did pay it. I brought back the ass and cart and Mrs. Crinegan told me to let him out in the haggard. She said, "There's only a small bit of last year's hay in the corner, and he won't do it any harm." I let him loose, hung the tackle in the shed, thanked her, and walked home.

Two days later the ass is dead. And while she doesn't come out directly and blame me, I can tell by the dirty looks she's throwing my way that she holds me to blame.

Later she admitted to Seán Rodgers that the ass had eaten ragweed and poison ivy and died from that. She said she never lets the cows or calves in the haggard for that reason. But she didn't think it would harm an ass. From there on in she started praying to the statues for an ass, but nothing seemed to be happening. Then she told Mammy she threw the lot of them out the window because they were no bloody good, and she prayed to the Blessed Virgin and got an ass. Now she says, "The Woman herself is better than the whole lot of them Saints put together."

Some tinkers going by one day sold her a black ass for four pounds, and she said, "This time I'll be more careful who I lend him to," while looking at me as though I have the plague. Later, she wanted me to help with some work, and when I said no she read me ten different directions, and said I'd never amount to anything.

I was trying to fix an old wheelbarrow Tom gave me, instead of the two shillings, and she came on the scene and called me a shit arse mechanic. She and Tom never got along, and I suppose when she heard I brought a load of turnips for him, she didn't like it. He says she has a tongue that would sharpen razor blades.

Speaking of razor blades, Tom used to sharpen the Max Smiles in a half glass of warm soapy water. He'd hold the blade against the inside of the glass with his two fingers and rub it around in a half circle till it was sharp. Mammy told him he should drink one pint of porter less and buy some, but he claimed he couldn't because they were rationed.

Tom seldom pays me what he promises. He still owes me the shilling he promised me for beating the tinker.

They were camped in the green at the bottom of the school wall. One of them about my age was across the road at the pump. Tom said, "I'll give you a shilling if you can beat him up."

I went over and asked him his name and he said it was Arthur and he was thirteen and a half. That was more than a year older than me. I hit him anyway and we start flailing away, right, left, and center. Pretty soon I realized he was tougher and stronger than me and beating the stuffin out of me. I broke loose and climbed up on the pump wall and he got up the other side, and we met in the middle of the high part at the back wall. The top of the wall is round with a lot of shiny moss on it, because it's in the shade of Ham's chestnut tree. The moss is all slimy and slippery. At the bottom of the wall in Tormey's field there is some rocks the council workers left when they were digging the well. There's also a mess of briers and nettles. We flailed away at each other again and this Arthur fellow swung a haymaker at me. I ducked just in time. He fell part way over and I gave him a good push. He fell off the wall and hit his head on a rock. He lay there in the briers and nettles for a while and I began to worry if he was dead, but after awhile he got up. Blood was coming from his head, and he said, "I won't fight anymore today, but next time I'll beat the shite out of you."

I decide to get out of there in case he changed his mind. I didn't come out too bad—I only had a black eye and a bloody nose, and it could have been worse. When I go across to the forge, Tom wouldn't give me the shilling, because he said that I didn't win it fair and square. I made my way home up past the green and the tinkers' camp, hoping his older brothers wouldn't come and beat me up. Instead a big stocky woman came toward me and asked if I was the young lad Arthur was fighting.

I say, "Yes, ma'am."

Then she says, "When I get through with him, he won't be fighting for a long time. I've warned him not to be fighting and bullying other children. Now young fellow, if he goes near you again just come to me and I'll take care of him, and I hope you gave him a few good licks."

I say, "Yes, ma'am, I did." I'm real happy with myself having started the fight and him getting the blame. When I get home, Mammy is none too pleased with me for fighting and getting my clothes dirty. She calls me a young gurier, and says she should have put me in a reform school long ago, but it's too late now, because "even they wouldn't have you. I'll give you something to do that will help to keep you out of mischief. You will go with Teresa and help her bring the turkey down to Brennan's."

I think to myself, here we go again. We did the same thing last year. When we get to Brennan's gate, Kathleen comes out and takes the turkey with its head sticking out of the sack, and the two shillings Teresa hands her. She leaves us standing at the gate while she goes to a shed where she keeps a whole lot of turkeys. She goes in and closes the door and comes back in about twenty minutes with the turkey. Teresa asks me, "Why does she bring the turkey in the shed?" I say, "I don't know, but Mammy said it's so she will lay eggs and hatch them and have young turkeys."

Kathleen Brennan went to school with my older sister Maureen and she was called "the jar of grease." Mrs. O'Kelly's husband fell

and hurt his arm and Mrs. Brennan sent in a little jar of goose grease
for him to rub on it. When Kathleen brought the grease to school, the
children called her "the jar of grease" and it stuck with her. They live
beside the Rowe's.

Pat Rowe is in the same class as me even though he is nearly two
years older. His brother Ned went to school till he was fourteen and
still couldn't write his name when he left. He got a temporary job
with the county council and when they asked him to sign for his
wages, he just stood there looking like a dummy. The man asked him
if he could write, and he said, "I can write Ned all right, but I can't
write Rowe."

Ned broke into a house and stole a fiddle and the guards went to
his house to question him about it. They asked him if he had the
fiddle, and he said, " I do."

"Do you have the fiddle complete?"

He told them he had the fiddle all right, but he didn't have the
complete. Thinking of Ned reminds me of a story my mother once
told me about a man named Innocent Mickey who used to go to
confession until the priest got fed up with him. He would say, "Bless
me, Father, for I have sinned."

"And what sin did you commit, my son?"

"I have no sins, Father." The priest got mad at him and told him
every man has sins, and asked him, "Do you curse?"

"Sure I just curse the devil, Father."

The priest said there was nothing wrong with that, "Sure I do that
myself."

Then Innocent Mickey said, "Feck him again, Father."

Then the good Father told Mickey he wouldn't have to go to
confession anymore.

Ned once told Pat Shanley he'd found a woman at last. "Red hair
and a pale face, a first cousin of my own, her name is Moll Cox. She's
getting her hair permed next week and I'm going half." The two of
them were sleeping in the fairy's fort in the field under a few sheets
of galvanized iron when Father Tom came on them. He brought them
up to the chapel, married them, and told them they could sleep where

they wanted now that he had them married. Her parents then took them in.

No one seems to know what the fairy fort is, except an overgrown stone wall in a big circle with trees growing out of it. Folklore has it the Vikings built it when they invaded Ireland. Mrs. Crinegan says she sees headless horsemen riding around it at night. I wouldn't mind what she'd say or see, she's not the full shilling that's for sure. And she hasn't a good word to say about anyone. Jim Finn said her husband died just to get away from her.

When Teresa and I get back home with the turkey, we find that Johnnie Dalton has been taken to the mental hospital. The ambulance came with three men and hauled him away. Everyone was expecting it to happen and wondered why it took so long. He'd been acting mighty strange of late, with a real meanness to go with it. He climbed the Nuns' bush in the bog when we were cutting the turf, found a pigeon's nest in it, and threw out all the little pigeons and left them to die. Mossy didn't like it, but he never said a thing to Johnnie. I suppose he knew he was about to flip. The Nuns' bush is a small tree in the bog on a little island. The reason it's an island is because the bog has been cut away all around it. The story goes that a priest and some nuns were murdered there when they were caught saying mass during the penal times. Now it's treated as a semi-sacred place.

I don't mind going to the bog with the Daltons. The first day on the bog we brought a clock so we'd know the time. We stopped for breaks at midday and another one later on in the afternoon. At those times we stuck some pieces of sticks in the ground to act as sundials. We set them so the shadow of one is in line with the shadow of the other. Next day when the shadows line up we know it's time for tea.

Usually, Mossy cuts the turf and I catch it and stack it on the barrows. Johnnie wheels it out and throws it on the lower bank or field where it will start drying. My job, besides catching the turf, is to build a fire to boil the kettle. It's not so bad at twelve o'clock because we bring the kettle full with water. Come afternoon, I have to go to the well out by the side of the road, which is half mile across the bog. The well water isn't very good and always has a scum of dust on it from the traffic going in and out the sand road. It took us two weeks to get Dalton's turf cut.

The evening after Johnnie killed the pigeons he had few drinks to relax, and then decided to take his clothes off and walk around without a fligget on him. Mossy had to go to the village and take him home. Shortly after that he tied the cat to the greyhound and let a rabbit loose in the field. The greyhound did what all country dogs do when they see a rabbit—he chased him, with the cat in tow. They say the cat only hit the ground here and there, with the dog making the odd snap at him. The rabbit got to the fence and escaped, and the cat survived somehow.

Next, Johnnie went to Mullingar, bought ladies' underwear, and brought them to the shop girl in MacAuley's and asked her to try them on for size. When she said, "No thank you," he told her she should go to confession and get rid of her impure thoughts.

When Johnnie's old motorbike ran out of petrol, he pushed it to McGuire's shop and asked Joe McGuire for some petrol. Joe told him he didn't sell petrol. Johnnie said, "Of course you do. You have petrol there on the shelf." He then pointed to a quart bottle of red lemonade.

"Be gad," said Joe, "if you think that's petrol go ahead," and he gave him the lemonade. Johnnie brought it out and poured it into the tank. He couldn't understand why the bike wouldn't start, then he told Joe his petrol was no good. Joe was getting a wee bit leery of him and didn't know what he might do next.

Patsy Rodgers came along and told Johnnie if he free wheeled the bike down the hill and kicked it in to gear it would most likely start. Johnnie got on, Patsy gave him a good push, and the last he saw of him he was below at Smiler Cormack's in the middle of the road kicking the motorbike.

Patsy told Joe, "Let him go to hell now and let the smart people in the village take care of him." He said, "They mind everyone else's business, now they can mind his for him."

Mossy kept Johnnie home for a while after that, but he couldn't control him anymore and finally had to call the hospital. They held him about three months, and when Mossy signed him out, he told Johnnie, "This will be the last time. If you ever have to go in again, I'll leave you there for good."

Patsy Rodgers doesn't like Moyvore since he got barred from MacAuley's for fighting. He's honest and tells people that he only fights when he's drunk, because that's the only time he has the courage. He and his father Joe, who he calls auld Rodgers, do the undertaking—or as they say locally, the laying out of the dead.

When Bob Mearse died, they had the job of laying him out. Patsy said they'd never laid out a Protestant before so they went in the pub for a few drinks to give them a little courage. When they got Bob washed and shaved, Mrs. Mearse gave them a new suit to put on her late husband. As Patsy told it later, he looked at auld Rodgers and the arse was nearly out of his britches, and here was a dead man going to be buried in a new suit. It just didn't make any sense, so he told his father to take his britches off and get in the new ones.

Joe had just dropped his britches down around his ankles when Mrs. Mearse walked into the room. She took a look at Joe and him with no underwear and ran from the room. Now Patsy didn't know what to do; he couldn't let his father wear the new suit because he knew they'd be watching them. He sends his father outside to the blind side of the house and dropped the suit out the window to him. Then he dropped the curtain cord down and Joe tied the old suit to it. Patsy put the old suit on the corpse, with the new shirt and tie. Then he put the Bible on his chest with his hands folded across it and a candle in the hands. Mrs. Mearse came in and admired the good job he'd done. Patsy told her, "Sure he looks great and very peaceful; sure he's like heaven on earth." He says, "He was a great man and always good to the poor."

He said Mrs. Mearse was very generous to him, and auld Rodgers wore that suit for years.

Patsy told this story to Smiler Cormack and I at the fire one evening. Smiler looked at him and said, "I think you're a better storyteller than an undertaker."

Confirmation

It's Confirmation day in Moyvore, and Anne and I are happy about that because we're the head of our classes. She's head of the girls' class, and I'm head of the boys. This means we'll be selected to answer questions for the bishop. Anne says the reason we're so good at religion is because there is always more of it in our house than food.

I sit at the end of the pew by the long aisle in the crowded church. I'm proud as punch with my hair combed and sleeked back from the soapy water in the basin at home.

The bishop and two priests are on the altar and Mrs. O'Kelly paces up and down the aisle, picking out the children for the bishop's class. She looks at me and ignores me and I get passed by while the other children go up to answer the bishop's questions. I feel a little bit disappointed. Then I wonder if it's because I'm wearing a jumper and all the others are wearing suits? But then Anne has a new dress and Mrs. O Kelly put her at the end of the class. And besides, I'm wearing a new jumper Mae Rodgers knit, and everyone in Moyvore knows Mae Rodgers is the best knitter.

At least Mrs. O' Kelly doesn't show me up like she did in school over my bad shoes. The bishop gets through asking his questions and we all go to the altar to be confirmed. The bishop comes, puts oil on my forehead and confirms me with the Chrism of Salvation, (holy oil) then he taps me on the jaw and makes me a strong and perfect Christian. Thankfully, it isn't a bit like the big slap on the jaw Anthony Tormey told me it would be, or the huge wallop that the bishop gave Liam Tormey that knocked out three of his teeth. Now I know it was all lies, and the bishop's big red face is not from bad temper. Suddenly, I'm not afraid of him at all, and I go back to my pew, kneel down, and say the bishop's prayer that Smiler Cormack taught me.

One in the morning is good for the sight.
Fourteen or fifteen between that and night.
Go to bed fasting free from all sin.
Get up in the morning and start it again.
Amen.

Back home, Mammy is telling Mrs. Keegan that Mrs. O'Kelly is one bad article, and she won't have luck for what she did this day, and she adds, "I wouldn't mind, but Paidin was the best one in the boys' class."

Then I know I'm going to hear some of the same diatribe I always hear when Mammy gets started. And right there and then my anger is fueled, and I vow I'll get back at Mrs.O'Kelly by hook or crook. I bide my time and it all comes to pass on the day we're getting out for the summer holidays.

Mrs. O'Kelly sits in a round armchair made from a kind of bamboo or cane type wood. She always wears a white blouse and a black skirt that's shiny from too much sitting. When she sits in the chair, she fills it right to the brim and sides because she's nearly as wide as she is long. A green velvet cloth covering the chair is tied to the four legs. I take four thumb tacks from the notice board and put them under the cloth sticking up, and she comes in and plops herself down in her usual manner. Now let me tell you, she lets out a scream and bounds out of that chair like a hunt horse going over a pole in a gap. Her face is all red and white and puffy, just like when the fire blew up her legs. She rubs her shiny skirt, looks at the chair, and then she runs out to the girls' cloakroom where she stays for about ten minutes. All the children in the class are dumbfounded and can't figure out what's happening. She comes back in, finds the four tacks that did the damage, and demands to know who did it. Nobody says a thing and she keeps looking at me. I think she knows well who did it, but I made sure I wasn't seen doing it, and I put a lot of thought and planning into my actions, so she can't prove a thing. It's Friday and we're getting out for the summer holidays. I won't have to look at her ugly face till school starts again.

A Letter Home

Our house is quiet for a short while after that, with just my mother and five of us left. Seán, Margaret, and Teresa have gone to Coventry, England, just like my other brothers and sisters. Eight of them have now hit the emigrant trail. When anyone mentions it to Mammy, she says, "What else would they do? Sure there's nothing for them around here."

Teresa finally got her wish to be out of what she called "this hellhole of a kip called Moyvore." I hope she's happy, because she deserves to be after all her efforts trying to feed us and keep the house going while Margaret, Chris, and Anne, went to school in Ballymahon. Margaret graduated with honors and was offered a job as the infants' teacher in Moyvore. Then Mrs. O'Kelly objected and said she would resign if Maggie Burke got a job in her school. What Mammy didn't say about that wasn't worth saying.

Father Tom told Margaret that if she insisted on taking the position, he'd give her his full support, but it could become a very uncomfortable situation. Margaret declined gracefully. In the meantime, Joe sent Seán the money for his fare to England. It was Anne who found his letter.

Joe Burke
Stoneystanton Road
Coventry
Well Seán ,
I hope you are keping well as this leaves me. They tell me you need a few pound for your fair. I got a cupil of shilins from the rest of them and am puting it in. You should hav plinty to get here. And we will meet yous at the trane. Let me know if you get the money. Sory about the pore righting.
All the best and God Bless,
Joe

Before she left, Margaret went up to Dublin to collect a statue of the Blessed Virgin for Mammy. I'm serving Mass when Father Tom tells me, "Your mother has won third prize in a raffle in Dublin." He says the prize is a thirty-inch statue of the Virgin, hands me a piece of paper with an address on it, and says, "Tell your mother the prize may be collected at this warehouse."

Frank had sold Mammy the ticket, which was for some sort of charity for the foreign missions. That was several months ago and Mammy couldn't figure out a way to get the statue down the fifty miles to Moyvore. So Dolly met Margaret in Dublin and they both went on a bus to collect the statue. They figured it wouldn't look right to be traveling all over Dublin with a statue in their laps, so they wrapped it in a blanket.

A woman on the bus approached Margaret and told her she shouldn't have the baby's head covered over like that, as it could smother. Dolly gave Margaret a nudge of her elbow and told her to be more careful. Then looking at the woman she said, "Don't worry, missus, I'll see she takes proper care of it."

Dolly takes a fit of laughing and tells Margaret, "You should be ashamed of yourself. The very first time you leave Moyvore you get in trouble. Now aren't you a right sight with a baby in your arms and you not married!"

Margaret gets embarrassed and her face is nearly as red as her hair. The woman goes back to her seat, complaining about the young mothers of today who have no idea how to raise children. She tells her friend, "Take that young redheaded one there? She'll be lucky if that child isn't smothered before the day is out."

Margaret gets the statue home and Mammy is delighted. She says if she won a million pounds, it wouldn't be as good. For a long time this statue stands on one of our best chairs in Mammy's room, until one day when I find a tea chest strong enough to hold it.

The Wagon

Frank and I decide to take the old trunk down to the forge and make a tinker's wagon. The trunk has been lying in the turf shed for ages; it was used for years to hold the family's clothes, until Teresa and Anne decided to throw it out. They said it looked too ugly without the round lid that was thrown out years before, and besides they told Mammy, "You don't need it now, since you have the wardrobe Watt bought you."

The trunk has a leather handle one on each end, and we carry it the way we used to haul the bucket of water when we were smaller. In the scrap heap at the forge we find an old baby's stroller that has seen better days and carried many a baby. It's all rusty, but the wheels are still in good shape. With a lot of effort and skinned knuckles we separate the wheels from the frame and attach them to the trunk. We turn the trunk upside down and lay the two axles across it. Next we make several holes on each side of the axles, and Frank gets underneath and pushes the wire up through the holes. We fix the axles in place by twisting the wire with the pinchers from the forge. When we think we have them well secured we turn it right side up, and it looks great. For shafts we use two ash suckers and fix them to the sides like we did the axles.

Now there's always a puck goat around Moyvore no one wants to claim because they smell so bad, and for some unknown reason they like to graze with cows. Today we find one in Tormey's field with the Kerry blue cow. After a long effort we manage to catch the goat and yoke him to our newly made wagon. We do this with reins we find in the forge. Now most tinkers' wagons have a round roof with a stovepipe sticking out the top. We have no roof for ours, but we do find an old three legged pot to act as our stove. When we get a good fire of turf burning in it, Frank gets in the wagon on his knees and I lead the puck out on the road and point him down the hill toward Smiler Cormack's.

Now if I didn't know it before, I know it now—puck goats are as stubborn as mules. Every time I let him go, he heads straight for the ditch. I bring him back up the hill and we start all over again, but this time I give Frank a stick to keep the puck's mind on his business. I take the goat by the ear and smig and run along side while Frank gives him a few licks with the stick. We get to a good gallop and I let go. And they sure look a sight flying down the hill with smoke coming out of this contraption. Then wouldn't you know it, no time would be better for Nora Mearse to come along on a fine hunt horse out the end of the green. I tell you that horse takes one look at that wagon and starts to do a well shod dance in the middle of the road. He shies all over the place. It reminds me of the times in the forge when Daddy used to hit the horses with the rasp to make them behave. Then he bolts for the green at a dead gallop and the poor woman doesn't have a hope in hell of pulling him up. Finally, he reaches the school wall at the far end of the green and digs his heels in. She sails over his head.

Now in all fairness to her, she holds onto him even though she is all shook up, with mud and cow shite all over her white blouse. By the time I get to her, she still seems a bit shaky with her legs spread wide apart propping her body like two braces to a fence post. Her light brown jodhpurs are stretched to the limit till I can nearly see the stitches in the seams. Now for some reason not clear to me I want to put my hand between her legs, but I know that would be the last thing I ever did. She would have me shot for sure. Apart from that, I know it is a mortal sin to touch a Protestant. Why even when passing their church on the road, I'd walk on the other side in case he with the cloven feet would come out and get me.

She slowly becomes aware of my presence and her eyes are staring at me like two bubbles in a piss pot. Then she lays a string of colorful curses on me like only a decent Protestant could. Now I am over thirteen years of age and sick and tired of older people pushing me around and telling me what to do. So I send a half a dozen of her own double "fecks'" right back at her. Then I decide to try out the two new words I learned in the village. So I call her a whore's melt.

Now I don't know what those words mean but they must've been fierce powerful, because she stands there with her mouth open in a state of shock, not believing any young whippersnapper would dare talk to her like that.

Her being Nora Mearse of the high and mighty, and thinks she's above all others in Moyvore. I leave her to her own dismay and go about my own business, hoping that would be the end of it. But it wasn't to be. Wouldn't you know it, she stopped at our house on her way home and complained to Mammy about me. Now if there's one thing my mother can't stand, it is cursing talk, or foul and profane language. Even Daddy for all he was, seldom used bad language.

Now here she is laying the broom handle on me real good and me trying to save myself. She swings it left, right, and center across me legs arms and legs and anywhere she can get a wollop at me. I grab the handle, and she shouts, "Let go of that broom." She is in a fierce temper and the knuckles of her hands are white from the grip. I haven't seen her so mad since she slapped Watt across the face for dropping his cigarette in the churn. He got thick and left and said he wouldn't be back. He only stayed away a few days much to my regret. Mind you, it was funny seeing her trying to fish the tobacco out of the half made butter.

She gives the handle a fierce jerk and I let go of it and she hits herself in the eye with it. Now she's going around the house with the dishcloth up to her eye, ranting and raving. "You won't have luck," she shouts at me, "for what you've done this day. God wouldn't be above but punish you and, your hand will be up in the grave for hitting your mother."

Now I'm beginning to get that auld horrible feeling in the pit of my stomach again. I can see auld Nick with his cloven feet, red eyes, and pitchfork ready to come and get me. Just about the time I feel I'm doomed, Maureen comes to my rescue. She tells Mammy, "He didn't hit you. You told him to let go of the broom and you hit yourself with it. Besides, what did you expect him to do? Just stand there and let you beat him over the head with it?"

Mammy snaps at her, "Who's side are you on anyway? And besides, he might as well have hit me as to what he done."

Now to cut a long story short, Mammy goes around with one of the finest black eyes ever seen in Moyvore. She tells people she walked into a door. But when going to Mass she puts a wad of cotton wool under her eyeglasses and says she has a sty in her eye.

Chapter Eleven

Fear

Christy Mahon asked Mammy if I could help him take some cattle to the fair in Ballymahon. He stayed in our house till all hours trading ghost stories with Mrs. Crinegan. One story was about six people playing cards, and one of them kept winning all the time. A player dropped a card on the floor and when he stooped down to pick it up he saw it was the joker. He looked under the table and saw the winning player had cloven feet. When he jumped up out of his chair, the one with the cloven feet went out the door in a cloud of smoke and there was a smell of sulfur left in the room.

I hardly sleep a wink after hearing that, and when I get up at about four in the morning I nearly had to pry my eyelids open. I make my way down through the village to the end of Egan's pub and let myself out the iron gate that hangs between it and Bob Mearse' stonewall. Fifty feet further on is another gate, and the space in between is used as a cattle pen. It is so dark I can barely see my hand when I hold it up. There's no moon and not even a star in the sky. I can feel the hair standing on the back of my neck and I imagine I see that fellow with the cloven feet. I try to make out the outline of the small path that leads through the fields to the corner of Puttingham Road. During that quarter of a mile walk, I keep listening for the slightest noise. A woodcock coos in the trees and I jump straight up.

As I pass the ridge of hills with all the yellow furz bushes on top, I recall the time they dug out the badger from Donald Rush's gravel pit. I hope he doesn't have a brother ready to attack me. Some people say badgers do no harm and should be left alone. I was very young at the time, but the picture stays with me. The men had five dogs, and they took turns fighting the badger in turn inside his den. The men kept digging from each side of the burrow till we could almost see the badger. Then they got a pile of furz bushes, set them on fire, stuffed them inside the burrow, and smoked him out. The dogs were all around him fighting, but the badger held them off till Patsy Mahon stuck a pitchfork through its belly and pinned him to the ground. The dogs then tore the badger apart and he made crying noises like a baby. I knew something wasn't right about it, and it brought a sad feeling to me.

Patsy Mahon is Christy's father and he was a ganger (foreman) on the council at the time. He often came to our house to get some boiling water for his tea. He'd sit Anne on his knee and tell her little stories, and she would pull his moustache. I thought he was a gentle man, but every time I saw him after that I remembered the badger.

I'm about half way between the village and Puttingham when I hear a chain rattle, and the hair stands on my head. Terror comes over me and it seems my heart is in my mouth, and I can hear it beating like thunder in a hay barn. I start running and crash into a young bullock who lets out a roar. I later found out it was only a young weanling who was probably just startled, and the chain was some bullock scratching against a gate that was chained to a pier. I don't know if I went through the gate, opened it, or jumped over it.

I get to Christy's and get the fire started. He sleeps upstairs in the loft and as soon as the kettle boils, I start pounding on the ceiling with the broom handle to wake him up. After some time he climbs down the ladder, puts four eggs in the kettle, and when they're boiled he makes the tea. He asks me not to tell Peggy he boiled the eggs in the kettle because he says she'd kill him over it. He says he couldn't be bothered looking for a saucepan. Peggy claims tea made from egg water causes warts. He says that's only auld pisreog (old superstitious belief). We eat breakfast, go down through the fields and round up seven heifers, and then head out with them for the Ballymahon fair.

The trip is about five miles and those heifers break out in to fields several times. By the time we get there I don't know if I'll ever see the end of this day. Ballymahon is one of the largest livestock fairs in Ireland and the town is packed with cattle. Although the population of the town is only half that of Mullingar, the main street is much wider. Some say Ballymahon has the widest street in all Ireland.

We find a space for the heifers outside a butcher shop and hold them there, waiting for a buyer. I can see sides of beef hanging in the shop and I wonder how long it will be before those heifers are hanging somewhere, and if they think about it. Luckily they're are all settled down and quiet after the long walk.

Groups of cattle mill about on either side of us; at times they're inclined to get mixed up and we have a job to separate them. Some cattlemen come by in their shitty Wellingtons, poke the heifers with their sticks, and talk prices with Christy while I try to keep the heifers from scattering all over the place. They slap his hand to splatter the spit and swear it's their final offer. Christy turns his back on them and declares he'd rather drive them home than take a price like that. I sure hope he doesn't mean it. I feel as though I could never drive those cattle all the way home again.

The church bell rings up the town and I start to say the twelve o' clock Angelus. A man guarding the cattle next to me says, "That's not the Angelus; sure it's only ten in the morning. It must be for a wedding or something." My heart sinks and I wonder if the day will ever go any faster than one second at a time.

Noon hour comes and Christy brings me a cheese sandwich and a bottle of red lemonade. I just get it down me when a jobber comes along and makes a deal for the heifers. Most of the selling and buying is done by this time, and the cattle and people are beginning to thin out. Christy gives me six shillings and gets me a ride home to Moyvore crossroads on the back of a tractor and trailer.

When I get in the house, Mammy asks if I've eaten and why is my hair standing straight up as though I had seen a ghost. I take the looking glass that's broken down the middle and peer into it. Sure enough, my hair stands straight up like a hedgehog's, and in the broken glass I can see two of me. I think to myself, there should be two of me. After all, I had enough fright for two and I owe a lot of it to that auld biddy Mrs. Crinegan and her ghost stories. Just the same, I think, why won't my hair lie down after nearly twelve hours?

I'd like to tell them about what happened, but I know they'd just sneer at me and make jokes about it. Me, Paidin Burke, who's never afraid of the dark like some of the others. Me, the one who beat the tinker at the pump and didn't get paid for it. Me, that wouldn't cry for Daddy and his leather belt, or for Mrs. O' Kelly and her stick. No, not me, I'm not afraid of the dark.

Village Families

The Burkes are the largest family in Moyvore. Next are the Tormeys and the Rodgers. And then, as Smiler Cormack, says there are the careful ones. Bill Tormey once told Daddy his children were the best fed children in Moyvore. Daddy had replied, "Why wouldn't they, and they having the fall of every table in it." Daddy and Bill never got along too well, and Mammy says it all went back to when Daddy was active in the I.R.A. He told Mammy he was going up to Scotts for a game of cards. Mrs. Tormey came running in to Mammy and asked, "Where's Joe going?"

"He's going to play a game of cards with some of the men."

Mrs. Tormey said, "Cards, my eye! They're all going down to Ballinacargy to ambush the barracks because the Black and Tans are having a dance in there and won't be expecting them."

Mammy ran to the forge and confronted Daddy about it. He called a meeting and told the men, "When every woman of the village can know my business, then it's time for me to quit." And he did. When the troubles ended, they all got pensions but Daddy. The government sent him an I.R.A. medal with an invite to apply for a pension two years after his death.

Teresa told Mammy she was entitled to the pension as his widow and should apply for it. Mammy answers, "Not if I were to starve to death would I take their lousy pension."

Teresa said, "We all nearly did several times."

Mammy goes on, "After all your father done for his country and he nearly being shot several times."

"Yes," said Teresa. " He sure did a lot for the country—like populate it, and all that."

Mammy ignores her and goes on to lambaste the traitors of Moyvore. "At least, thank God he didn't live to see his sons go to England like the Tormeys."

The Tormeys are a little bit older than the Burkes and they were the first family from Moyvore to start the trail to England. People say the coastal counties of Ireland are nearly deserted due to emigration. Mrs. Crinegan claims this is because the land there is poor and can't support families; there's better land in the midlands and the people aren't as desperate for jobs. Seán Rodgers says, "One could have said that a few years ago, but not today." He claims the tractor has taken over. "Sure, it's doing the work of six men. Look at James Keane just above the road. He had six men working for him and now he's down to only two. He has a machine now that's called a reaper and binder and it cuts the oats, threshes, and spits the straw out to the side all at the same time. Now how could any man compete with that? I'm telling yis the machine has put paid to work."

Mae Rodgers thinks it's because the people in the outer counties don't have as far to walk to the boats, and the people inland are waiting for transport. Smiler Cormack says the country's going to hell and the people with it.

Mrs. Byrne calls in and asks Mammy if she ever saw anything get as lonesome as the whole world. She had to close down her little shop at the hill of Skeagh for lack of customers and she claims people are leaving for England "by the new time."

Egan's store has closed down for the same reason. Some say the manager John McPhillips was sacked for selling his own stock instead of the company's. They were out on the street saying their good byes and Mrs. Mac cried her eyes out. Mammy said it was a pity, she wasn't the worst of them, and she hated seeing her go. Mrs. Mac and Mammy were good friends.

Egan's put in a new manager and he got Chris and Anthony Tormey to clean out the storeroom. They brought several loads of stuff down to the bog and burned it. There were cardboard boxes with hundreds of packets of cigarettes that had all turned brown. They smoked them all day till they got good and sick. Chris never could light a fag after that without getting sick. Egan's changed hands several times after that. Then Liam MacAuley bought it and sold the liquor license so another pub could never open there.

The village has gone very quiet and the "pitch and toss" is nearly gone. It used to be a big part of the weekend, with as many as twenty or thirty men playing. They'd place a round stone called a spud on the road and then pitch two pennies at it from about twenty feet. The nearest penny to the stone was left where it landed, and the other one taken up. When everyone had pitched their penny, the closest one to the spud got to toss all the coins into the air two at a time. At times heated arguments would start over who was the nearest. A piece of stick or straw would be used to measure the distance of each coin from the spud. Then they would be placed on a flat piece of wood or a pocket comb tails up, and the tosser would throw them as high as he dared. Sometimes there would be a lot of betting on the outcome of the toss. Some would bet on them coming down heads, while others bet on tails or harps. The one tossing gets to keep all the heads, and the tails are left for the next nearest the spud.

Meantime, someone has to keep a lookout for the priest. He says it's gambling and should not be practiced by any decent thinking Catholic. "Not," he tells them, "that any one of you are decent Catholics." When he walks along reading his office, he's easy to spot, but one time he pulled up in his car out of the blue and kicked the spud and the pennies all over the place. The following Sunday he read all their names from the altar and gave a strong sermon on the evils of gambling. They all got very religious for a while after that and went to confession. Then a new place had to be found for the pitch and toss, away from the prying eyes of the priest.

A Bunch of Liars

Joe is home from England. Himself and Seán came home from Coventry at Christmas, and he decided to stay on. Seán had some sort of English accent and everything was "co blimey" this and "co blimey" that with him. Anyway, he spoke some sort of foreign tongue seldom heard around Moyvore. Joe told him to cut out that auld stupid talk or he'd blind him all right. Seán only stayed two weeks, as he had to get back to his job. He works in a foundry, whatever that is.

Joe is having too much fun to think of going back. He plays football on the Moyvore team and they want to keep him, as he's their best player and the leading goal scorer. Pat Shanley says Joe's a team on his own. He gets a few days work here and there and with the little he has saved, it keeps him going—or so he says. Most of us think it would be better if he went back. That way the money would still be coming into the post office like it does from Seán and Watt. I like it when he's around because he still has a wicked temper and gets in fights when he has a few drinks. He always wins.

Himself and Seán had a few pints of Guinness in the pub before Seán went back, and Joe brought home a steak to fry for himself. He left it on the pan beside the fire to go out and talk with Mike Lee, the postman. They were old friends and had a good chat, but when Joe got back in the house his steak was gone. He asked Seán if he'd seen the steak and Seán said no, he hadn't, but he saw the cat a minute ago. Joe ran out and caught the cat at the end of the house eating his steak. He grabbed the cat and stuck it in the barrel of water to drown it. He had him under water for a while when Seán came and gave him a good push and the cat made his escape, tearing Joe's hands in the process. He washed the steak off in the barrel and began to fry it.

Mammy told him he couldn't have luck eating meat on Good Friday. " Be Janey," he said, " I didn't know it was Good Friday, but now as I have it half fried I'm going to eat it anyway. And besides it's a good Friday that I have it to eat."

Frank brings home a magazine called *The Far East* with a little box to collect for the black babies of Africa. Joe says it's all a joke because when he went to England, the black babies' parents were driving cars while the arse was out of his britches.

Joe got in a fight with Philip Schaffrey in the village, and Philip comes to our house to make the peace with him. Joe's getting into bed when Philip comes into the room and asks Joe to shake hands with him and forget all that happened. Joe says, "I'd shake hands with any man, but you aren't a man." Philip had been in the pub saying something about Nanny (Tom's wife) and didn't know Joe was behind him. Joe tapped him on the shoulder and asked him outside. Philip told his listeners, "This will only take a few minutes," and he followed Joe outside. When Joe threw a punch at him, Phillip got cowardly and ran away.

I'm lying in bed listening to their arguments. "Now, Joe, you know I respect your mother and your father, God rest him, was a great friend of mine. Will you shake hands with me for their sake?"

Joe said, " I'll tell you what I'll do, I'll give you till the count of five to leave this house, and if you aren't out by then, you'll be carried out."

Joe starts toward Philip, who decides it's better to leave. He tells Mammy on the way out, "I tried, Mrs. Burke, and you know it. God knows I tried, that's all a man can do."

Shortly after that Joe tells Tom he ought to keep his wife at home and not have her making eyes at every man in the village. They're about to get in to a fight, but Mammy gets between them. The next day Nanny's at the crossroads shouting over at our house. "You Burkes, yis think yis are king shite, but yis are not. Yis are just a bunch of no good liars the whole lot of yis, and yis are all inbred bastards, and yer father before yis was no good, that's why he died above in Dublin rotted away from cancer, and ye with the nerve to tell everyone he died from ulcers. Ulcers how do, but then come to think of it, lies is nothing new to the Burkes, yis are all a bunch liars."

"That's it," said Joe. "I'm going to kill that bitch."

He goes out the gate and Mammy shouts at him to come back,

"Come back, Joe, you'll only get yourself in trouble, and she's not worth it."

But Joe doesn't hear her. He heads for the crossroads and Nanny sees him coming. Well, let me tell you, you never in all your life saw a woman get on her bike so fast. She was a quarter mile up the Mullingar Road before he gets to the cross. I know she was fierce lucky he didn't have a bike, because if he caught her I think he might have killed her—and I believe she knew it, as she'd seen his temper before. Further to that, Joe's the one Burke she's really scared of. Her father told Tom that even he could never control her.

I heard Mammy remark that she couldn't understand how Tom got hooked up with someone like Nanny. That was about the closest Mammy ever came to saying anything about her woolly lamb.

When it comes time for Moyvore to play Ballymore in the final, they put Joe on as sub, and give his place on the team to Eddie Ham, a prominent farmer. At half time they're losing by five points, and they beg Joe to play. Andy Hughes says, "Don't you dare go on, Joe Burke. You were good enough to win every game for them and now when it comes to the final, they put you on as a sub. Let them go straight to hell, them and their snobbery."

They lose the match, and are drowning their sorrows in MacAuley's pub when Jimmy Ham remarks, "We'd all be drinking from the cup tonight except for one man, and that man is Joe Burke." They get in a fight and Liam MacAuley calls the Gards, and they come to arrest Joe.

He tells them, "Look, ye are a pair of old men. Go home before I hurt yis."

They say, "That's alright, Mr. Burke, we'll be back for you in the morning."

Joe's thumbing a lift to the boat next morning at seven o'clock. He goes back to Coventry where he continues his fighting ways, and he didn't set foot in Ireland again for many years.

Back from England

Maureen is home again with her two children. This time she says she'll be staying for five or six months while her husband finishes the house he's building for them. She comes and goes so often one would think Coventry was just down the road. She is, as Chris says, "a right pain in the arse, and one would think she was the only one ever to have a baby the way she fusses over them." The oldest one's name is Carmel. She's three years old, and the baby Gerald is six months. She feeds him a formula called "Cow and Gate" that we have to get in the chemist in Ballymahon, and I am sick and tired of going for it. Just about every Friday she waits for the money to come in the post so she can buy this food for the baby. Anne asked her why doesn't she get in a supply of it and not have that baby crying and whinging all the time with hunger, or better still she said, "You might try feeding him the old fashioned way. Or are you too grand for that since you went to England?"

The two off them go at it hot and heavy and Mammy has to separate them. Maureen gives me four pence for my effort and it works out to a quarter penny or a farthing a mile. I make sure and spend the money as soon as I get it, because if I don't, I can rest assured Mammy will take it off me like she does all the money I earn. Here I am over fourteen years of age, and not a red penny to show for all my work with the farmers all summer. I'm beginning to understand how Teresa felt, and I have this kinda feeling in me, a sort of an emptiness and a longing—for what? I don't know.

All I really know is I want to get away from everything, and I just about know that one day I'll leave like all the others. I know there are places beyond Moyvore and Mullingar. I got a puncture and had to walk most of the way from Ballymahon and Maureen gave out hell to me for being late with her Cow and Gate. That did it. I told her she could stick her four pence up where Biddy stuck the rent, and from then on she could go for it herself.

Mammy picked up the broom to go at me again for my poorly chosen words. I told her straight out she wasn't going to hit me again, and for some reason she backed off. The only one who gets to keep his money is Chris. He works for Bob Mearse and he's determined to keep most of what he earns. Then again, he's is a good bit older than me, and he can do that. Mammy tried to take it all from him the first week, but he just wouldn't give it up. I can't say I blame him. He says he'll be going to England soon to do his apprenticeship as carpenter, and I can't blame him for that either. He says Maureen's husband, Mike Rowland, is getting him in with a builder and he'll get to wear a white shirt and tie with a pencil behind his ear. He did two years in the technical school in Ballymahon before going to work for Bob Mearse, and if he can do it, so can I.

Anne told him, "I hope it stays fine for you with your big ideas, you bloody eejit." She's forever mouthing off at someone, and Maureen says she has a disease called diarrhea of the mouth.

Speaking of diarrhea, it was my last gift to Mrs. O' Kelly. I boiled a whole bunch of Mammy's Senna pod leaves and added the juice to her tea kettle. She said good riddance to me when I left, and I was glad to see the last of her. I hope she had a free weekend.

Anne nearly got in trouble last week with Mammy for talking back to her, and she ran outside and kept knocking on the door. Each time Mammy would go to answer it, Anne would run away. She kept this up till Mammy got so vexed her face was white with temper. She called out to her, "Don't you worry me, young lass, you'll have to come inside before this day is out, and then you know what will happen to you." Then Mammy got the basin of dish water to throw on her, and she told me, "When she knocks next time, you pull the door open real fast and I'll let her have it."

We wait inside the door till the knock comes. I pull open the door and Mammy throws the basin of water out—not on top of Anne, but on top of Father Tom, who was calling to see her. Mammy got fierce flustered and embarrassed and her face was all red. She says, "I'm so sorry, Father. I thought you were Anne, and I didn't mean to throw it on you. Here let me dry you off." She starts wiping him down with her dirty dish towel and it's only making things worse.

He throws up his hands with his prayer book in one and he says, "For God's sake, will you leave me alone, woman!" He turns on his heels, and walks out the gate, and heads for home. Mammy was so ashamed she could talk of nothing else for days, and Anne was forgotten about.

The Jock

I'm well into my first year at the technical school in Ballymahon when Father Tom comes on the scene and asks if I'd like to become a jockey. Now whether I would or would not makes no difference as far as I am concerned. One doesn't say no to the priest, so my answer is, "Yes, Father." To go with that, I kinda like the idea of becoming a famous jockey and making lots of money.

This starts another short episode in my life. Anyway, I'm not doing very well in school, because they're into algebra and all other types of things I never learned working for the farmers. English, okay; the woodwork shop, okay; a spattering of Irish, okay; but algebra? Forget it!

Multiplication is vexation.
Long division is just as bad.
But the rule of three puzzles me,
and fractions drive me mad.

"Drop him off at the church in Kilcock," is Father Tom's instruction to the Board Na Móna lorry driver.

"I sure will, Father," came the reply from the fat man behind the wheel. So it seems as though the drivers don't say no to the priest either.

Turning to me, Father Tom says, "All you have to do is wait at the church gate and you'll be picked up."

I wait and wait, from eleven thirty in the morning until three thirty in the afternoon. I'm freezing with the cold and dare not go into the church out of the wind and rain in case someone comes and I'm not there.

A shop across the street has chocolate bars and sweets in the window, and boy would I like to get my hands on them, but as usual I haven't got a penny in my pocket. It reminds me of the time I was catching the turf for Tom Cormack and the two boys his sister Maggie took home from England.

Two children not much younger than myself appear on the scene all dressed in fine clothes and shiny shoes. And there was I like a scruff bag, with scabs on my head and my arms all caked from the dried turf. I wanted to play with them, but I knew I couldn't. I wanted to ask them for a piece of those red Chivers' Jelly bars they were eating, but I knew I couldn't. I was there to work, to do a job, and I thought of what my father said when he jerked the bellows to wake me up. "Remember what you're here for." I think of all those times when we children would stand at the table while Daddy ate his steak and potatoes with our tongues hanging out, each one of us hoping we're to be the one favored with the bone. Or when he'd have his eggs for breakfast and each one hoping for the top of it till Mammy would pull us away by the ear and tell us to, "Let your father have his meal in peace."

Now here I am, forty miles from home with not even two pennies to rub together, and hungry as ever, and what do I do if nobody shows up? My mind runs in all kinds of directions and I'm dreaming up different kinds of calamities when a motorbike makes a u-turn on the street and pulls up beside me. The man takes off his cycling glasses and asks if I'm the one to be picked up. When I answer yes, he says, "My name is Master Joe Robinson and you may call me Master Joe, Mister Joe, or sir. But if you call me anything else, I'll break your head."

Now I can think of a lot of things to call the bastard right then, but I'm much too cold and miserable and wet to say anything. So I decide to keep my tongue in my cheek for the moment, knowing full well that he'll never be my master, not till the day he dies, the fucker.

He says, "Jump on," and we speed away. I am so cold I only pray

I can hold onto his black leather coat that I know is waterproof, unlike mine.

"I run the farm, and my younger brother, Master Willie, and my sister Miss Lynn work at the horses. You'll be working for them. You just do as you are told and we'll all get along just fine. By the way, what's your name?"

I can barely hear him over the wind and rain and the sound of the bike. He asks again, "What did you say your name was?"

I don't want to answer him, but I don't want to get off to too bad a start either so I say, "Master Pat Burke."

"What did you say?"

I repeat, "Master Pat Burke." I know I can't back down now or I'll never live it down, and he'll always be pushing me around.

There's silence for a minute, and then he says, "I'll tell you, Master Pat Burke, you're lucky you aren't going to work for me on the farm, because if you were, you'd be dead in a week." No more is said as we travel the five or six miles to Robinsons of Larch Hill and my future.

The head man in the stable is Anthony Flynn, and he shows me how to groom and care for a horse. Then I'm put in charge of three of them. This entails taking them out for their daily exercise, grooming them, cleaning out the stalls, and giving them water and feed. Fourteen horses occupy the stalls and five more are out on grass. Of this five, three horses belong to Father Tom. One is a mare in foal; one is a four-year-old gelding trying to overcome an injury, and the other is a two-year-old colt. The head stable man takes care of four horses and there's also an older man who goes around blowing spit from his pursed lips as though he's trying to sooth a horse all the time. His name is Peter Calaghan and I'm told he was quite a good jockey in his heyday. One of the men told me Calaghan got his blowing impediment from a fall late in his career. He cares for two horses. Willie Robinson, who's two years older than me, or Master Willie as I'm supposed to call him, cares for two more. Everyone has their own job.

My living quarters are in a small room adjoining the stables, with a bed, a small table, and an enamel washbasin and bucket. The stone walls are whitewashed and a light bulb hangs from the ceiling. I get my meals in a little hallway off the kitchen at the main house. I'm not allowed inside the house or kitchen. After eating, I have to wash the dishes in the outside scullery and leave them back. One week rolls into another and Christmas comes, and I get a piece of Christmas cake to go with my dinner. I lie on my bed and already I'm beginning to have those old lonely feelings of emptiness, of wanting, of needing, of home, of things different. Spring comes and the yellow daffodils are in the ditches and we've sent only four horses to the races. The best result we get is a third place finish.

Master Willie rides a horse called Royal County and he pulls him up at the first fence. Anthony Flynn said I should have ridden him and he nearly got in a lot of trouble for his remark. I feel I might not have done well either, but I do know I would have made a better effort.

We have a four-year-old mare that refuses to be broken and is always chomping on her teeth. Anthony Flynn takes her down the field with a halter and throws her. He has me sit on her head while he beats her with the hunting crop for three or four minutes. When we let her up she stands with her legs spread wide apart, trembling like a leaf. He puts the bridle and saddle on her with a tight martingale and I give him a leg up. She lets him ride her just like she knew what it was all about. Unfortunately, she jumps into a ditch a few weeks later when hunting, hurts her back, and has to be put down.

Mr. and Madam Robinson give me a lift to Mass in the car some Sundays. They never speak a word to me going or coming, and sometimes I wonder if I have the plague or something. He's a cross old so and so and goes around as though the weight of the world is on his shoulders. They say he was a captain in the army and had to buy his way out of it.

We get a winner at Naas racetrack with a horse called Sunny Star, and Madam is in the stands shouting for all to hear, "Look at the way he's beating my horse." That's the most I have ever heard her say, and thankfully Jimmy Eddery the jockey doesn't hear, so we get the win in spite of her.

My birthday comes and goes, and I'm fifteen years old for five days before I know it—not that I can celebrate anyway, because I'm broke. What else is new? I was promised a half crown a week, and so far I've gotten it only twice.

Five of us decide to cycle to the races at Fairyhouse and Anthony Flynn lends me sixpence. Instead of buying sweets, I bet it on Cottage Rake. When he wins at twenty to one, I feel as though I am rich. I give Anthony Flynn two shillings for the sixpence he lent me and after buying lots of goodies I still have six shilling when I get home. And that's more than all the wages I have got for the past seven months.

Joe Robinson asks me to help him move some cattle down the fields, and when I say, "Yes, Joe," he gets all mad and huffed at me. He pushes my arm up behind my shoulder and keeps asking me to say, "Master Joe."

I hold out for a good while, but I finally have to give in and say "Master Joe."

Now for some unknown reason I wake in the middle of the night and stroll down the yard. There in the generator room is Joe's motorbike. It's the only motorbike in the place, the only motorbike to get both wheels flattened, and the only motorbike to get piss in the tank. I wasn't picked on again after that.

Anthony Flynn takes me with him to Ballydoyle races with a mare called Joanstown. We really fancy her chances and I put my last three shillings on her. She's sitting in third and makes a lovely move to the front, and then breaks down. Anthony and the driver of the horse box stop on the way home for some drinks, which takes over an hour while I wait in the horse box trying to sooth a hurt mare. When we get home, Mr. Robinson is waiting with the vet and what he doesn't say to Anthony wouldn't be worth saying.

Now I'm back where I started: flat broke and as poor as the day I arrived, and I begin to wonder what the hell I'm doing in this place. I would be as far ahead if I'd never left Moyvore.

It's decided to geld Father Tom's two-year-old colt. Anthony Flynn leads him down to the field with Mr. Robinson and the vet. When the job is completed, Mr. Robinson tells me to bury the results. I start to walk toward the stables and he calls me back to ask where I'm going.

I say, "I'm going for a shovel, sir."

He says, "Don't mind the shovel. Pick them up and take them with you, and then get the shovel."

So here I am forty miles from home heading for the stables with the balls of Father Tom's horse in my hands, and I feel that old shame and anger and rage boil up in me again, and it's just like the time when the cock crew at me when I had to empty the piss pot. I think of a lot of things I'd like to say to the Robinsons, to the Masters, to the Misters, to the Sirs, to the Madams. My mildest wish for them is that they may all die roaring without the priest.

Next day I give Mr. Robinson a few seconds notice. I say, "I'm leaving, sir. Goodbye."

"Come back here!" he shouts after me.

"You go fuck yourself, sir!" And I keep on walking. I walk to Kilcock, and one of the same Board Na Móna lorries drops me off at the Moyvore crossroads. So here I am, fifteen and a half years of age, one year older, a little wiser, and just as broke. I went there with nothing and I came back with nothing, and I now understand it was never meant for me to become a jockey, but to give my free labor to help pay for Father Tom's horses. Anything else I might say about that would be at the cost of my soul. After all, the priest is not to be messed with. He is, as my mother would say, a holy man, a man of the cloth.

Chapter Twelve

Cancer

Lilly Rodgers is very sick in the hospital. Her brother Seán came in to see Mammy yesterday and told us, "It's not looking good. They transferred her to the cancer ward over a week ago." He added, "You know, Mrs. Burke, no one has ever come home from there unless it be in a box."

Mammy says, " I know, Seán. It's too bad, and you know we all like Lilly."

"She asked me to ask you if you'll go in to see her. She says she'd love to see you, Mrs. Burke. I have never heard her ask to see anyone before. She must be fierce fond of you, missus."

Mammy says, "Sure I'll go in to see her, and is there anything I can bring?"

He says, "She doesn't need a thing, except maybe you could bring her a few fags. You know she's a divil for them woodbines, and they say they're the worst kind. I'm thinking of quitting them myself."

Seán has a job with the county council cleaning the roads. We can hear him coughing in the morning going to work. He says, "It's that auld flim in my throat." Mammy tells him he aught to go to the doctor about the cough, but he says, " I already did and the doctor told me to give up them cigarettes as they'll give me a slow death. That's exactly what I want, Mrs. Burke—a slow death, I'm in no hurry. But to put all coddin (kidding) aside I will have to give them up, because I know they can't be good for me." Then he says, "You know they don't try to stop her smoking in there anymore. I suppose they think it's not worthwhile. Not that she's able to smoke, but if you do bring her a few woodbines, it would let her know that people are thinking of her. You know, just a little something."

Mammy takes me with her to Mullingar to see Lilly, as she thinks I was Lilly's favorite. This is my second time to go to Mullingar on the bus. I remember a lot from the first time, but it isn't raining like before. Daffodils grow by the side of the road and the bushes are white from the May flowers. Near Shandonagh Bridge I recognize the place where trees and bushes grow out over the road from each side to form a tunnel. It looks as though the bus is too big to get through. Then I remember the Board Na Móna lorries go this road all the time and they are taller than the bus.

Mullingar isn't very busy. There aren't any cattle on the Main Street and it is clean. I see the railing where I threw the ice cream and I again wish I hadn't done it. Margaret brought home some ice cream from Ballymahon one time and it was grand and soft and not too cold. Mammy says more people are getting richer by the day, as there must be nearly twenty cars in Mullingar whereas there used to be only nine or ten. She says, "It must be well for some."

We get to St. Mary's Hospital and Mammy asks for Lilly Rodgers at the desk. A nun with a big white hat that looks like a bishop's hat, tells us to go down to the end of the hall and turn right. "At the end of that Hall you'll come to a door on the left and that's where Lilly is." She tells Mammy we can only stay about twenty minutes because the doctor will be making his rounds.

The hallway is lined on both sides by a wooden rail about three and a half feet high. Above it the wall is painted yellow, and the underneath is painted a light shiny green. The rail is painted a dark shiny green like the doors. The place smells of disinfectant. Mammy says she thinks the smell is Lysol or pine. I know it doesn't smell like Jeyes fluid. Half way down the hallway we pass two big doors that go right across the hall. The bottom is wood and the top is glass. I wonder what good the doors are if you can see right through them. They don't have any lock and they swing either way. We pass through them, down the hall, and find the door to Lilly's room.

Inside the small room, a little old wizened up woman lies in the bed. Her eyes are sunken in her head and her cheekbones stick out like two big hand knuckles. She has dark rings round her eyes and I can count all the bones in her hands, as though the skin can barely hold them together. Mammy stands by the bed looking at her for nine or ten seconds. She asks, "Is that you, Lilly?"

The little old lady opens her eyes and in a feeble voice that's barely a whisper, she says, "Hello, Mrs. Burke."

I stand at the end of the bed because I'm scared to get any closer. Mammy asks, "How are you feeling, Lilly?"

Lilly responds, "I have good days and bad days. I'm feeling much better today and if I continue to improve I could be home inside a week."

She sees me at the end of the bed and asks, "Is that your boy, Mrs. Burke?"

Mammy says, "Sure that's Paidin, don't you remember him, hasn't he always been your favorite?"

Lilly turns her head slightly as though trying to remember. She holds up her hand a little bit and I know she wants to touch me. I want to stay at the end of the bed, but Mammy says, "Come and shake hands with Lilly."

My heart thumps and I feel a kind of a shiver all over me. Mammy takes my arm and brings me to the side of the bed. As I take Lilly's hand, all I can feel are cold bones. I make sure not to squeeze it in case it falls apart in my hand. I want to run from the room, but I know it wouldn't be right. Mammy keeps trying to talk to her, but she falls in and out of sleep. We hear the doctors coming and Mammy leans over her and tells her we're all praying for her. I don't know if she ever heard it.

Out in the hall, Mammy leans against the wall trembling and says, "Paidin, just give me a minute and I'll be all right." I've never seen Mammy so quiet as on that trip home.

I want to tell someone about it, how Lilly Rodgers was all bones and looked like a witch, and how she scared me, but I don't.

I think back to the time when Daddy borrowed Farrell's pony and trap to bring us to the sports in Abbeyshrule. Lilly said, "Joe, I'd love to go to the sports, but I have no way of getting there because auld Rodgers took the bike to go to the bog. Is there any chance you could give me a lift?"

Daddy said, "I don't know, now let me see. There's Margaret, Teresa, Bunny, Anne, Paidin and myself. That makes six in a small trap.

Lilly says, "Sure, Paidin can sit on my lap and I can mind him for you while you have a few pints in McGoey's."

All seven of us headed out for the sports in Abbeyshrule, about three and a half miles from Moyvore and on the river Inny. I enjoyed the clip clop of the pony as we went down the rock road past Pearsetown and Williamstown and on to Abbeyshrule and the sports. Daddy paid our way in at the gate and took the pony and trap over the bridge to McGoey's pub. There were all sorts of things going on, from three-legged races to tug of war to horse races. They had a tent with round targets and pellet guns on a counter.

Another tent had slot machines and a round red and white wheel a man spun. A big table was piled with apples, oranges, sweets and chocolate. I was hungry, but I had no money so I couldn't get anything. When a man bought an orange and peeled it, I picked up the skin and started eating it. It burned my lips around my mouth and I decided I didn't like oranges.

A jockey fell off a horse going through a gap and blood poured from his nose. He got up after awhile and said he was all right. On the far side of the river a long pole stuck out over the water with a large ham hanging from the end of it in a sack. The pole was all greasy and the sack had big knots in it. People in swimsuits paid for a chance to walk out the pole and get the ham. None of them could do it because they kept slipping and falling off. One man got all the way out and it looked as if he was sitting on the ham, but he couldn't untie the knots. Finally he too fell off.

Lilly bought a hand full of bull's eyes for me. I didn't see the others, and I figured they've gone down to the other field. I was pleased about that, as it meant I didn't have to share with them. Several hours go by and by then I was starving with hunger.

The last thing to take place is the long swim—men have to swim from the greasy pole to the bridge. By then, Daddy was back with us, standing on the bank smoking his crooked pipe. The swimmers clung to a thick rope stretched across the river until they heard the whistle, and then they all started to swim. One man fell behind and he kept going up and down, trying to get over to where we were. Daddy kept saying, "That man is drowning!"

He stood near the bank and a man went into the water up to his waist. He grabbed the swimmer and pulled him to the bank. Daddy stood over the man, rolled him onto his back, and pumped his stomach for what seemed to be hours and hours. Finally, milky colored water came from his mouth and after awhile he started to breath and sat up. Daddy got us back in the trap and we headed for home. He let us out at the house and said he was going to leave the pony back.

A few days after our visit to the hospital Lilly Rodgers died. I try to think of her as I knew her years before at the sports in Abbeysrule and the times she would give me piggy back rides and how she could get around Daddy and save me from his temper. Then I think about that awful word cancer and that face in the hospital always comes to the fore, and I would see it for many years in the darker corners of my mind.

A Visitor

There's a new boarder in our house: Granny Gibney has come to stay with us. Our grandfather, Tom McCann, died at the age of forty-six, leaving Granny with two young children to rear. She then married Jim Gibney, who didn't take kindly to having two young children in the house. Aunt Maggie, who was eleven at the time, came to live with us and went to school in Moyvore. Uncle Tommie went to live with our Aunt Nellie when he was about nine years old. When Granny's second husband died, she sold their small farm and went to live with her younger daughter, our Aunt Nellie. And of course, now that all her money's gone she comes to live with us.

We all think Granny is great and we enjoy listening to her old-fashioned sayings. She and Mammy sleep in the big room, and Anne has the box room all to herself. Frank and Eddie sleep together and I have a bed all to myself. We've come up in the world to the extent that there are new springs and mattresses on the beds, and the house seems warmer. Anne still has her job working at the post office for Massie Cormack. She teases Mammy a lot and they have grown very close. I think it's because she's the only daughter left at home.

One day, Anne was sitting by the fire eating toffee and Mammy said, "You mean little faggot, you wouldn't even offer you own mother a sweet."

Anne gave her a toffee and Mammy seemed to have a lot difficulty chewing on it. Anne started laughing at her.

Mammy said, "You and your old toffee, you can keep it. She went to throw the toffee in the fire and her false teeth went with it. "Now look at what you made me do!"

Anne grabbed the tongs, but by the time she got the teeth out of the fire they were just about ruined.

She held the tongs up in the air for all to see, with the blackened teeth and the toffee running down it, and she couldn't stop laughing. Then she sobered for a moment and said, "Let's get this straight, Modleen. I didn't make you do anything. You asked me for a toffee and I gave you one."

"No, I did not! I asked you for a sweet, and you should have told me it was toffee." Anne couldn't stop laughing. Mammy looked at her teeth and said, "Sure they're entirely destroyed." Then she added, "Maybe it's just as well, I never could get used to them."

Anne took her to Mullingar and had them replaced, but Mammy never did wear her bottom set of false teeth again.

I haven't gotten much work since I came home—just a day here and there. Then I got six days with Mick Brennan on the bog. Mick is a nice quiet, strong man who lives with his crippled mother. She's confined to a wheelchair and he has to do everything for her, including putting her to bed and getting her dressed. His sister took care of her for years until she went off to make her own life. He leaves everything ready for the dinner before we leave in the morning, including a pot of potatoes, and bacon in another pot. He leaves them hanging on the crane, and she's able to swing it in and out over the fire with her walking stick. He leaves a big basket of turf beside the fire where she can reach it, and she's able to throw it on the fire.

Mick cuts the turf, I catch it, and Patsy Rodgers wheels it out with the chestnut mare. Although he's quiet, and never swears, Mick loves to talk about women. He never had a girlfriend in his life that anyone knows of. Patsy is as good a storyteller as ever and any chance he gets he regales Mick with stories of his great conquests. This slows up the work a little and makes the day go faster.

Then the topic switches to Patsy's recent adventure in undertaking. "I heard you had a little trouble laying out John McLaughlin," says Mick.

This is a sore subject with Patsy and he doesn't want to talk about it. The story goes that John, a big heavy man, died in a sitting position. Now Patsy, having had an unusual amount of drink for courage, decided to lie down beside the corpse and he fell asleep. He awoke at some ungodly hour of the morning shivering with the cold. When he couldn't straighten out the corpse, he went and got Pat Shanley to help him. Pat got on the chest and Patsy on the lower area and they started to heave. The end of the bed broke down and Pat Shanley and the corpse fell on top of Patsy. He shouted in a wild panic, scrambled out the door, and wasn't seen again for weeks.

"Well devil the bit of trouble," says Patsy. "Sure I got a fierce dose of the flu and I had to go home to bed where I stayed for two weeks."

Mick goes to the house to put on the cabbage and we follow him up a little later. We let the mare loose in the field for about three quarters of an hour. After dinner, Patsy gets the job of catching the mare. He puts some oats in an old basin to coax her. Now I know well that Patsy isn't too keen to catch her to go back to work. So when she comes to him, he throws up his arm wildly and says, "Whoa there, mare! Whoa there!" The mare shies away from him and takes off down the fields in a gallop. Mick is standing beside me and says, "Pat Burke, will you just look at him the way he's frightening the mare. Now I ask you, is that man an eejit or is he not? Now that does it. From now on you'll catch the mare."

When I tell Pasty about it on the way home, he gives me fair warning not to catch that mare for at least half an hour. Now him being older and bigger than me, well I'm not about to argue with him.

Next day when the mare comes to me I say, "Whoa, there, Whoa, there," and give her a good prod in the nose with the safety pin I borrowed from Mammy's sewing box. Boy, oh boy, does she ever take off. It took Mick the best part of an hour to catch her after that. Later on Mick stands in thought and he says, "You know, Pat Rodgers and Pat Burke, between the pair of yis, I am a demented man."

We get the turf cut early Friday and Mick tells us he found a whole nest of hen eggs in the hay shed, and we're going to have eggs instead of bacon and cabbage. Patsy knocks the head of his egg first and there's a chicken in it. We go outside and I nearly get sick. After awhile Mick comes out to say he put on other eggs to boil and he knows they're good because he had some last night. But I couldn't look at an egg for weeks after that. Other than the eggs, I can honestly say that even though the work was hard, we had some fun and I enjoyed it.

Nothing of interest happens around Moyvore for a while after that. I'm just hanging around the house and going for the odd hunt with Spot. Some evenings I sit at the fire with Smiler Cormack, listening to his old time sayings and stories. He had a pair of boots with holes in the soles and Matt Rowe suggested he should take them to the cobbler and have new soles put on, because they were worn to the last. When the Smiler got the bill for them, he remarked, "It'll be a long time again before they go to the last."

The Suit

Sam Connaughton ordered a new suit from the tailor in Ballymahon. This came about on some friendly advice from his good friend and neighbor, Matt Gibney. The latter told Sam it might be a good idea if he got new clothes and have a good clean up and shave as a surprise to his wife. So on fair day, Sam yoked up the horse and cart, went to Ballymahon, and picked up his new suit.

On the way home he stopped at Burnett's and tied the horse to the iron gate and made his way through the fields to the Puttingham river to have a wash. He stripped off behind some bushes where he stowed his new suit for safe keeping. Going to the river, Sam threw his old clothes in and let them float away. Then Sam got in the river with a bar of sunlight soap and did what he hadn't done in years—he washed himself. All was going well until he got back to his starting point and discovered his suit was missing. The only things left were his boots and greasy hat. After a long time searching, Sam gave up and made his way back to the horse and cart. He kept close to the ditches, with nothing to cover himself but his hat. The cart held a pile of straw and a green rubber water cape. Now this cape had no sleeves and was meant to cover the upper body area. Sam put on the cape, hunkered down on his knees, and pulled the straw around himself to keep out the cold.

He made his way up to the pub in Moyvore, where some young fellows were hanging around for the lack of something better to do. Sam shouted in at the bartender to bring him out a glass of whiskey before he froze to death. Drinking it down, Sam set out for home and reached the Ballymore Road before he realized some of the smart young fellows had set fire to the straw in his cart. So there he went— galloping toward home, flailing away at the smoking straw with his hat. When Pat Shanley saw him, he said with his cape flying up and down, he looked like the Angel Gabriel trying to take off.

Sam set out to give his wife a surprise and I'm sure when she saw him, she got just that. Me, I can't guarantee the facts of this happening, as I only heard it second hand. But Seán Rodgers says it happened exactly as stated, and that's what I'd have done, for sure and certain.

Mary-Split-the-Wind

I'm on my way home from Ballymahon with a mantle for the Tilley lamp that Watt bought when he sold the cow. Other than the light at McAauley's, it's the only decent light in Moyvore. The Keegans say they can see the Burkes' light from their house, which is a mile away. If they don't see it, then it means we're out of paraffin oil. I get as far as Bob Mearse's house at the end of the village and George Scally, Philip Murtagh, and Pat Murtagh are blocking my way and calling me Jock.

George took over Chris's job when he went to England, and the two Murtaghs are helping him draw in the hay. I try to go around them, but they grab the handlebars of my bike.

"Let go of that bike," says I.

George says, "Why don't you make me let go of it?"

"Ok then, so you want fight, is that it?"

Now what he doesn't know is that I learned quite a bit about boxing in the stables. I get off the bike and he swings a haymaker of a right at me that would knock my head off if it connected. I duck it nicely and come up over it with a right that connects squarely on his right eye. I can feel the pain go up my arm. He goes to one knee and I lay another on him. I turn to the Murtaghs and ask if they'd like to try their luck.

They say, "No, it isn't our fight."

George asks Pat Murtagh, "Is my eye bursted?"

I tell him, "No, it isn't, but it will be if there's a next time."

He never bothered me again.

When I get home, Mary-Split-the-Wind is drinking tea and smoking by the fire. Mammy thinks she's a bit innocent and suspects she's in the family way. Her real name is Mary Murphy and she's in training to be the priest's housekeeper. She came to Moyvore a few months after I left for the stables and is engaged to some farmer from up near Killbegan. She volunteers to get down the lamp from the ceiling and when she gets up on the chair to reach for it, it becomes obvious to Mammy that her time is near. Mammy asks her if she goes with any fellows and Mary says, "No, I have my own man waiting for me."

Then Mammy says to her, "You wouldn't do anything foolish, would you, Mary?"

"Oh! God, no Mrs. Burke, sure I'd cut my own throat before I'd do anything wrong like that."

Now for a short time this is a conversation piece for the holy Marys, and Mrs. Crinegan, who says, "It's a prime example of the young people of today with their lack of morality." She can't understand how it could happen, especially when Mary was never seen with any man. But then she opines it will be just another virgin birth in Moyvore.

She goes on to say, "It won't be quite as bad as what happened to the young Shanley girl." This occurrence happened many years ago, but I've heard it so often it seems like yesterday. Apparently, the Shanley girl went to the doctor and he discovered she'd given birth, but she insisted she didn't. He had no choice but to tell the authorities and they found the dead baby under her bed, wrapped in a coat. Then the fine elders of Moyvore decided she would not be prosecuted if she left Moyvore and never returned. They said they didn't want the shame of it to fall on her family, her father being a prominent person in the community. Why he might even lose his job over it. So at the prime age of sixteen she went to England and was never heard from again.

We only saw Mary-Split-the-Wind a few times after that, and then she was gone. We heard later the farmer refused to marry her because of her condition, but changed his mind when her parents offered him a good-sized dowry.

A Dead Hen

"Ah! Sure God, missus, I can't give you anything for that hen, sure that hen is dead." Jimmy Connell has a little shop near Abbeysrule and he also drives a horse and four-wheeled cart to Mullingar every Friday to the market. He buys potatoes and vegetables and poultry from the locals and sells it at the market. Now Mammy tells Frank it's time we got rid of that old hen we call Pluckeen.

Frank brings out the hen, legs tied and all, and offers it to Jimmy, who tells him to put it on the ground. Frank puts the hen on the ground and it decides to die right there and then. Once again, Mammy is—as she says—mortified with the shame of it all. "It wasn't you know as if I'd set out to sell him a dead hen."

Frank declares that it wouldn't matter if the hen was dead, if we'd killed it, that is. But the thing is it decided to die all of its own accord and could have had a disease. Then he says, "It must have died from fright, or maybe Daddy sent for it to keep him company."

Mammy tells him to watch his mouth. Anyway Jimmy Connell doesn't know if it died from a bad disease or not, and you can't sell dead poultry at the mart like you can rabbits.

I've set out a good plot of cabbage plants in the garden and Jimmy says he'll buy them from me when they're ready. He says cabbage plants are going three and six pence a hundred, and I'm already counting my money. I can hardly wait for them to grow. I intend to have a bit of money in my pocket now that I'm smoking. I started a few weeks ago, and I get four woodbines in a green open end packet for three pence. Every spring we buy cabbage plants if we can find some. So I got the idea to sow some seed and have plenty of plants in the spring. I fenced off a nice piece of the garden and tilled it, and now I'll have plenty of cabbage plants for sale. Things are looking up.

The Bathroom

There's no bathroom in Moyvore, not that anyone knows of anyway, so Donald Rush decides to build one and I am his helper in attendance. How this comes to be is not unusual. I'm on my way from Ballymahon and Donald is standing at the yard gate. He tells me the potatoes are near boiled and adds, "Why don't you come in and have a bit of dinner with us?"

Now he has a good way with words, as well he should have, seeing as how he does more reading than working. My brother Joe hung around with him off and on and said it wasn't unusual to see him and his wife Vera sit each side of the fire reading while there was work to be done, and the cows bawling at the haggard gate waiting to be milked. But I gladly accept his offer, and I go in and help them dispose of the extra food most farmers feel the need to cook. This is in case, as they say, company shows up—and if that should happen then it's just too bad for the dogs, they'll have to settle for the skins. After all, the laws of hospitality must be adhered to. After eating to my heart's content and taking some good draws from the butt of a woodbine, I decide to leave. Having stayed for what I think is a respectful amount of time, I head for the door saying a well heard thanks. Outside, with my hand on the latch of the yard gate, Donald asks me would I mind giving him a hand to mix a few bags of cement to finish the floor of the cow stall he's just built. This takes us a little over two hours, and then he tells me of his plans to build a bathroom over the large back porch. This idea really whets my appetite. Here, I think to myself, is a chance to see something built—a real bit of building. The only thing I've ever seen built was a shed Daddy and my older brothers put up years ago, and the straw roof of that was leaking in no time. Now I know Donald won't pay me very much for my effort, but it will get me away from the house. And what if he only gives me fag money? It will fit in nicely with other things I have in mind, and I can give a few days work to the other small farmers in between.

Now most people in Moyvore and areas beyond know Donald was never cut out to be a farmer. When Pat Farrell died, he left him the farm well stocked and tilled, and Pat was so tight with money he squeaked when he walked. Some even claimed he still had the Christening money he got when he was baptized as a baby. For that reason alone, the locals figure a lot of money went with the farm. Most of the heavy farming changed when Donald took over, and now he just keeps a few cows and a small number of sheep. He does just enough tillage to keep the house and a couple of pigs, and saves enough hay for the cows and the mare. Now this same gray mare wouldn't pull the flies off a dead rabbit. I find this out later when I take her down to get a load of gravel from the pit where the men killed the badger years ago, and she's barely able to pull a small load.

My brother Tom, who shod her a few times, tells me she's more hunt horse than a workhorse. That being the case, it's my intention to give her a few good workouts. The rest of the land Donald has set out to other farmers by the eleven months. I ask why eleven months and I'm told the other month gives the land some time to recover.

Things are going along just fine, plans are taking shape in my head, and life is looking good for me. There is great talk of this bathroom. Mammy and Mrs. Crinegan don't understand why Donald and his wife need a bathroom, especially with only the two of them and one small child in the house. They decide they're just copying the Americans, who they say have a bathroom in every house.

I'm on my way home one evening when Mrs. Dalton comes along, riding her twenty-seven inch man's bike. Just I am wondering where she might be going or what the mad auld bitch might be up to, she heads the bike towards me and swings off it beside me. "Paidin," she says, "when you see Donald Rush, tell him to come and take back that shotgun he lent to Mossy." Then she says, "You know Mossy has been in St. Loman's three times, and there's no telling when he might go off the head again and kill us all."

I say, "I'll tell him, missus." I turn my bike around, head back down, and tell Donald. Now if ever I saw a man really worried, he is just that. He just doesn't know how he's going to get that gun back from Mossy. He pleads with me not to say a word to anyone, and I tell him my mouth will stay shut, especially if I have the price of a cigarette to put in it. He takes the hint and gives me money for woodbines. He gets the gun back a few days later by telling Mossy he has to take it in to the barracks to have it registered. So all's well that ends well. Donald has his gun back, I have my woodbines, and the Daltons are safe.

My father's annual memory Mass comes and is attended by the remaining five of us. The five years seem to have flown by, spring is fast approaching, and the disaster happens.

Arthur Mearse's cattle break into the garden and eat all my nice cabbage plants, I grab the first thing I can lay my eye on, which happens to be a pitchfork with one prong broke off it. I run down the garden screaming at those big whiteheads, but I can see it's too late, because what they haven't eaten they've trampled into the ground. I'm so vexed I just whale into them right, left, and center, and I only wish I had that shotgun of Donald's. I get them back over the fence and as the last one is going over I stick the pitchfork in his belly. He goes buck leaping across the field and it must be fifty yards before the fork falls out. I look at the mess where my lovely plants had been, and I just stand there in utter frustration. There go my plans and my future, the plans I'd worked so hard for. I'd cared for those plants like I would a baby. I covered them with bushes and straw all winter to protect them from the frost, and for what? Just to have them eaten by those blasted cattle. I intended to buy a ferret with the money from those plants and make real money. That's all gone now and I'm back to where I started, just baggy arsed and broke. I wonder if Father Tom put a curse on me for not staying at the stables to help pay for his horses.

As soon as that thought enters my mind I get rid of it, because I don't believe in the power of the priests like the rest of them. Apart from that, he got another free job of work from me since then. I helped Pat Byrne drive his cattle from the railway at Castletown in the middle of the night and I never got a sweet thank you for my effort that took five hours. And I wonder if the words "thank you" are missing from the priests' dictionary, because they never seem to use them.

I get on the nine foot iron gate in front of the house and rattle it in temper for about twenty minutes, but the only thing it does is put pain in my arms. I just hang around the house for the next couple of days, licking my wounds. I go down to Donald Rush and he has the greatest of sympathy for me. He tells me if I do a bit of work for him on and off, I can sow three drills of potatoes and three drills of turnips with him, and can't I get a few suck pigs come early winter, and wouldn't it be a good start? So the deal is made in the manner of gentlemen, without a handshake, and we start working on the bathroom.

We pour a small foundation round the porch and bring a six inch wall up the sides. When we get it up to the cement roof of the porch, we break off the four inch overhang and let the new wall in over the roof another four inches, so from there on up the wall is ten inches wide. A cock pheasant crows down the fields, and Donald asks for quiet that he might figure out what direction it came from.

Now if there's anything Donald likes more than reading, it's shooting, so we drop everything and go for a shot. Five hours later we get home with one measly pheasant to find the bag of cement I mixed in the morning has gone hard. The building slows down for awhile, because we're busy doing the tillage and cutting the turf, but mostly because of lack of money to buy cement. I give Christy Mahon a few days doing odds and ends and all he can talk about is the bathroom. He wants to know if I'll give Vera the first bath in it, and is it true what he done when they first got married? Apparently Donald told someone he sewed the blankets to the mattress on Vera's side of the bed so she couldn't get away from him till he got his marital rights.

I tell Christy, "I doubt if Donald needs my help to bathe Vera," but in my mind's eye I can picture it as plain as daylight. As for the marital rights, I have a fair idea of what that means, and the feelings it brings to my body are pleasing for sure. I tell Christy I heard the same story, but it's not something I'd risk asking Donald about. Vera is a very pretty woman and would be the pick of Moyvore if she hadn't come to it already married. Both Christy and Mick Brennan love to talk about women, and neither one of them will ever see fifty again.

We meet Frank Mullins, and Christy asks him for the loan of a clocking hen. Frank says he doesn't have one. Christy says, "You had one a few days ago, I saw her myself." Frank tells him the clocking has gone off her. "Well," says Christy, "that's a holy fret, and where are you off to this early in the day, Frank?"

"Ah! Sure, I'm going to the doctor, I've had a bad case of the mourn (constipation) this past long time, all I can do is marbles."

Christy looks at him in a quizzical sort of way and says, "That might not be so bad, just look at the goat in the field. All he does is marbles and isn't he the healthiest animal in it?"

Frank says, "By gad you know you're right at that, I never thought about it like that. Sure it's only too healthy I am," and he turns around and goes home.

We get Donald's tillage done, and the roof of the bathroom is ready for pouring. Every piece of steel or iron we can find we put into it, but it isn't enough. Then I remember the axle of the ass's cart in the forge. Donald's eyes light up when I tell him about it. It's two axles welded together, end for end, that Tom had made as a wench for Kenny's mill before it closed down. The contraption has been laying there for years going rusty. Now Donald can't go for it with the mare and cart, because he knows well that Tom won't let him have it till he pays for work already done. And if I go for it, Tom will be inclined to give me a good clip on the lug.

We're giving some thought to this problem when Pat Rowe comes along riding a bike, and before long Donald has talked him into helping us. So it's decided that Pat and I can bring that axle with two bikes when Tom isn't about. We tie it to the carrier of his and attach it to the handlebars of mine at the rear, and off we go down through the village. When we get to the top of the hill at Egan's we decide to ride the bikes the rest of the way, it being mostly downhill to Rushes.

Now all is going well until a lorry comes facing us. Just as it passes, we get too close to the ditch, the bike wheels start to wobble, and we lose control. At the bottom of the hill is a small bridge with a stream running underneath where Daddy used to shoe the wheels before he got the water pump in the village. At the last second I slap on the brakes, but it's too late—we all come crashing down: bikes, axle, the lot. I wind up sitting on my arse in the stream and it would be so funny if it weren't so close to disaster.

Pat lies on the bottom of the pile, with the bike on top of him and the end of the axle stuck in the ground right beside him, and he's lucky that it didn't go through him. One of his elbows is badly skinned and the front wheel of his bike is bent and twisted. Then he tells me his bike had no brakes, and I could malavogue him (beat the hell out of him) him right there and then.

Now we're left with only my bike, so we load the axle on it by sitting it on the handlebars and tying it to the carrier, and we walk one on each side to balance it. This works out well, and Pat says we should have done it this way to begin with. We get it to Rushes and Vera puts a bandage on Pat's arm. Donald tells him to bring him the bill for the bike repair and he'll pay it.

I think to myself, some fat chance of him paying for it, and if he does, it will be a first. More than likely it will be like the time he promised me the puppy from his little fox terrier. When she was in heat I took her over to Mick Brennan's terrier and mated them. Donald promised me the pick of the litter, but when they were old enough to sell or give away, he got rid of all of them and I was left with the smallest one, a bitch at that. Now a bitch might be okay around a farmyard, but around a small council house forget it— especially when male dogs come around barking at night.

Still she was a grand little dog, and growing quite nicely till Frank took her down to the village and she got run over with the wheels of a Board Na Móna lorry. I'm sure he thought I was going to beat the hell out of him for it, but I never said a word, because by that time I had gotten used to disappointments.

I was working on the bog for Tom Cormack when Donald brought me the news. He was very disappointed that I didn't show more concern, but like the shadows of the past that day is gone, and a new one comes and here we are pouring the roof of the bathroom. We start it early in the morning and I've never worked so hard in my life.

We mix the cement two bags at a time at the strength of three to one. Donald stands above on the deck, pulling it up a half bucket at time while I mix it and fill the bucket. When it's all gone and I start to mix another two bags, he says he wants to check on something in the house and he doesn't come out again till I have it mixed. By this time I'm beginning to think he keeps going in to get his marital rights. I am fast taking a dislike to Donald Rush, and I'm finding out he isn't a man to be trusted, because he never keeps his word.

He promised me three drills of potatoes and three drills of turnips and I wind up with just two of potatoes and one of turnips, and even they won't be there unless he mends those fences. Himself and Mossy Dalton work together since one of Mossy's horses died, as it takes two horses to do tillage or mow meadow. They made a deal with me to catch their turf, drop their potatoes, and weed Donald's turnips, and they in turn would cut the turf for me. Well, when the time came, they gave me one lousy day on the bog, and that was just about five hours. Then Frank and I had to cut the turf all by ourselves.

Mammy said they couldn't have luck for it, but she expressed surprise at Mossy. My thoughts for them weren't so mild, the pair of fuckers.

We get the roof three quarters of the way finished and Donald says his hands are too sore from the rope, and I'll have to carry the rest of it up the ladder. We get it done anyway and he's hoping the rain won't come and wash it away. If it does, I couldn't give a shite, because I'm so tired I could sleep for a week.

Chapter Thirteen

Anne Leaves

Anne has gone to England, and she's the last of the Burke women to immigrate. She said she got fed up washing Massy Cormack's slimy snot rags and dirty smelly socks. She was supposed to be working as assistant postmistress, but that only happened when there wasn't housework to be done. In the heel of the hunt, she wound up doing both jobs and she said enough was enough.

Before she left, Anne read a postcard that came in for Philip Schaffrey. It was from Tom's wife Nanny, and it read: "Philip, Come up to see me Tuesday evening. Tom will be gone off to shoe a horse."

We didn't really know what it meant. Who knows, maybe she wanted to borrow some money from him for cigarettes or something. Anyway it was a topic of serious conversation for a good while in our house. Granny told Anne she could get herself in big trouble for telling people the contents of someone else's mail, and could be had up for it. Anne replied that she couldn't give a damn, as she'd be in Coventry, and if the powers that be wanted her, they'd have to come there and get her.

Next day at Mass after the sermon, Father Tom reads the list of the offerings for the upkeep of the parish. "James Keane—one pound, Eddie Higgins—one pound, Paul Rooney—fifteen shillings. Mossy Dalton—ten shillings," and so on down the line to the smaller givers, "and Mrs. Burke—two shillings." Then he pauses for a special announcement:

"Tomorrow, Monday, is the drawing in of the hay for the parish, and all those who wish to help please give your name at the door."

I think to myself, parish my arse, what he means is for himself not the parish. Anne nudges me and asks if I'm going to leave my name, and I tell her, "I will in my arse, I think he got enough free work out of me."

At home Anne asks Mammy why we give more to the collection than James Keane, who's a big farmer. Mammy says, "What do you mean? James Keane gave a pound, which is ten times more than us."

Anne says, "Now let me see. James Keane has nine hundred acres of land and we have a half-acre. So according to my reckoning, he should be giving eighteen hundred times more than us."

"Glory honor and praises to God and his holy mother," says Mammy, "But you're a walking mathematician, and what will we ever do without you?"

She would have her chance to find that out two days later when it came Anne's time to leave, and she did. I felt a sense of loss, knowing how much I'd miss her. I wanted to tell Anne, but I couldn't.

Mearse's cattle brake into Rushe's tillage. They are eating and trampling the turnips, and Donald is running after them trying to get them out. James Finn comes sauntering along, chewing on his gums and Donald tells him he'll get a fucking electric fence to keep those cattle out. James agrees it would be a good idea. "Either that," he says, "or repair the fence you've got."

I wonder how he can have an electric fence without electricity. I suppose he could get a big generator like they have at Robinson's, but then he has no tractor or belt to turn the flywheel. He must, as my mother would say, be doting.

Next morning the same thing happens again, Donald running after the cattle trying to get them out of the tillage. James asks him, "What happened, Donald? Did you forget to turn on the switch this morning?"

Donald tells him, "Fuck off. You and your smart aleck remarks."

Donald's gray mare is always breaking out and going up to join Bob Mearse's two bay horses. Donald doesn't mind that—he says, "Sure it's free grass for her, but I'm the one who has to catch her when we have a bit of work."

That mare is the cleverest bitch that ever walked; she lets me get close to her and then bolts. I pull the old trick with the oats in the basin, and nab her. I put the bridle on, climb on her bareback, take her down the big field, and do five rounds of it under a strong gallop while I lay the stick on her. I let her ease down and she's trembling like a leaf. A day of hauling stones for a gap and she quits her wandering ways for a while after that.

I hang around the house for about a week watching the hay carts drawing the hay for Father Tom. Then I decide it is time to clamp our turf, and Frank and I go to the bog. And wouldn't you know it, some son of a bitch set the bog on fire and some people lose their turf. We're lucky the fire didn't come our way, but it put a bigger rush on us to get it saved and home.

On the way home we stop in to see Tom Cormack and I ask if he'll lend me the pony to draw the turf out to the road. He agrees, in exchange for me helping with theirs. Tom and his brother Ned are two bachelors living in a typical two-story farmhouse. They never miss Mass, nor do they leave the house without dipping their fingers in the holy water to bless themselves. Last time I worked for them, Tom was about to bless himself at the door when a mouse ran across the floor. He just had his fingers up to his forehead when he spotted it, and shouted, "Will yis look at the fucking mouse."

"My God," said Ned, "will you not be cursing in front of the garsún" (young man).

"I wasn't cursing," said Tom.

"You were cursing," said Ned, "sure I fucking well heard you!"

And that was most of their talk done for the day.

Anne told me one time that Tom Cormack was in competition for Mammy's hand, but he lost out to Daddy. I wonder what difference that would have made in our lives, or would we be here at all, and would I ever have got involved with Donald Rush?

We work hard to get the turf saved and brought home. Two trailer loads with Darby Mahon's tractor and trailer, for which we pay him two pounds a load, and at least we won't have to be rooting in the ditches for sticks this winter, and I can turn my attention to digging out the potatoes. I haven't been down to Rushes' in a while, so when I go down the field, I'm not prepared for the sight that confronts me. Just about all my turnips are eaten and the two drills of potatoes are trampled into the ground. I stand there in frustration, with anger welling up inside me. Here I am again—all that work and nothing to show for it. I'll be lucky to get enough potatoes to see us through the winter, and I decide right then and there that some people are just about two arms and two legs worse than useless.

I think about what Mick Brennan said to Patsy Rodgers: "Between the pair of yis, I'm a demented man." And now I understand how he felt, because right now between the priests, the Protestants, and the farmers, I am a demented man. But we live in hope, and Mammy says God is good, and He never closes one door without opening another.

A few days later I'm on my way home from Ballymahon and I meet Jackie Burnett. He went to the technical school with Chris and he started making wooden gates and selling them to the local farmers. Jackie is a real nice type of fellow, considering he's a Protestant, and not like those high and mighty Mearses with their noses turned up at the less well off. We just dally to have a few words, when across in the field near the bog I spot two foxes playing. Now I know there's a nice bounty on foxes, so next day I bring the crowbar, a spade, and Rushes' terrier and go after them. As luck would have it, I dig out seven foxes. The government used to pay for the tail of the fox, but too many local dogs wound up without tails. Then they tried the ears and then the tongue, finally settling on the head. So I use Vera's favorite bread knife to cut the heads off, and I bring them to the barracks in Ballymore. I sign the form and the Guard asks to take a look at them. When I open the bag he looks in and turns his nose up in disgust.

When I get back, Donald says, "I suppose they kept the heads?"

"No," says I. "He told me to throw them away."

"Throw them away? Do you think you could find them?"

Right then and there I know what he's up to, and I'm sorry I told him. In the next few minutes we're out in the shed trying to start his old car—a vehicle that up to now has seldom been driven anywhere except to Mass. As per usual he takes the easy job of sitting inside and pulling the choke, or whatever he does, while I wind up the crank. Five minutes of this and she starts. Off we go for the fox heads.

He took them in to Ballymahon and collected on them. Someone said Seán Rodgers also collected on them, and where they went from there no one knows. But I'm sure those heads went from barracks to barracks till they were rotten. Meantime, I get my potatoes dug out and brought home, and that was the last of my trucking with Donald Rush or his bathroom. And no, I did not get to bathe Vera.

The Ferret

Now here I am with the turf in for winter and enough potatoes to last till next spring. Most people would be happy to be in my position. But not I, said the rabbit as the dog chased him. I need some money in my pocket. I'm considering going to Mullingar to try and get a job with the county council when word comes that my ferret has arrived at the railway station in Mullingar.

I sent for it two weeks ago to Enniskillen in County Fermanagh, with the bounty money I got for the foxes. So I make my way to the station and pick up my little yellow ferret. He comes in a square wooden box a bit bigger and in the shape of a loaf of bread. And so my new project begins.

All is going well and I'm back in the woodbines again. Mick Connell buys the rabbits from me once a week and I'm really getting good at this ferreting. One week I had eighty rabbits, and if I can keep it up I'll be able to take the hill of Halston for trapping. When Watt had the ferret, he used a line on him and he was always getting it wrapped around roots in the burrows. Watt would spend hours digging him out. I put a muzzle on my ferret, set nets at the burrow openings, and catch the rabbits in the nets when they bolt. I usually leave two openings—one for Frank to watch and one for myself.

Seán Rodgers came with us a few times, till one day he put in his hand to pull out a rabbit, and he swore that the rabbit bit him. Now many a person had bit into a rabbit, but I swear I never heard of a rabbit biting back.

Seán is in all reality a professional coward, and when he played football he'd run and leave the ball if he heard steps behind him, in case he got hurt. Seán lost interest in ferreting that day, and I must say it was just as well, because Frank and myself did just fine on our own. Spot chased a rabbit over to the yard of Paheen Ahearn's little house at Cnoc Na Boy, and he went in under a flagstone in the yard. We block off all the openings we can find, put in the ferret, and in seconds the noise is like thunder. We start lifting the flagstones where the sound is coming from and we take out eleven rabbits. In all, we wind up with twenty-six for the day.

Now carrying that many rabbits is no easy task on a bike, even when they're panched, which means taking the guts out and cleaning them. We put a slit in one of the legs and put the other one through it and hang the rabbits on two crowbars attached to the saddle and handlebars of the bike. Then, like Pat Rowe and I did with the axle, we get one on each side to balance it.

I give a few rabbits to Mae Rodgers in the evening and she asks me to stay for tea. Paheen Ahearn comes in and I get up to leave, but she asks me to stay awhile. I know she doesn't want to be there alone with him. Seán went in to Mullingar to get some clothes for their sons, Frank and Joe, who are upstairs in bed. After awhile they start shouting down, "Mammy, is Paheen gone?"

She answers, "No, he is not."

About every five minutes the same question. "Mammy, is Paheen gone?"

She gets fed up listening to them and she says, "Yes, he's gone," and they break into song. "You all know Andy Round Legs who smokes the fancy pipe, he smoked with Mary Dinegan sitting in her camp."

"Oh no, no, he's not gone!" shouts Mae, but it's too late, and Paheen drops the tobacco he's cutting for his pipe and heads for the stairs, penknife at the ready.

Mae shouts, "Oh no, Mother to God, Paidin! Stop him! Stop him!" Paheen is nearly halfway up the stairs and I pull his two legs from under him and he slides down to the bottom. Now he's trying to crawl up on hands and knees, and I pull him down again. This goes on for a little while and I say, "Paheen, this is getting us nowhere. You know well the childer didn't mean it, so why don't you sit down and have your tea?"

Now Mae, when she sees I can stop him from climbing the stairs, gets real brave and tells him he will behave while in her house or he can leave. He's white in the face with a dribble coming from his mouth, and puffing for air. Then he looks at Mae and says, "You give me two options, and I'll take the decent one and leave. No decent man would stay in a house like this."

I say, "Goodnight, Paheen." He says, "Goodnight to you, Paidin Burke, and bad cess (bad luck) to the rest," and he leaves.

Things are going along quite nicely, and I'm looking ahead to better things, when once again fate reaches out its black hand. Rabbits are dying all over the place and cannot be given away. They lie in the ditches and the fields with their heads swollen like footballs, and the eyes seem about to pop out of their heads. Smiler Cormack made a good meal from one of them before someone told him they had a disease.

Yes, the government in all its wisdom introduced a disease called myxomatosis. This disease was invented in Australia to combat the rabbit population, which was so numerous they'd destroy many acres of crops in one night. The Irish government, who in the opinion of many are just a bunch of wealthy farmers, decided the rabbits could ruin some of their crops and had to go. If they'd asked the common people, they would've learned that the meager rabbit is a good source of food for poor people who can't afford to buy their beef.

So here I am again—broke—with few prospects and an idle ferret. I remember what my father said, "Trust the government to get it wrong." I put my little yellow ferret in the pocket of my torn topcoat, bring him up to the hill of Halston, and set him free.

Tea Boy

What does one do when one's horse goes lame? Take him to a vet, and if that doesn't work take him to Joe Burke, or so Daddy claimed. But what does one do when they need a job? Go look for one—and so I do. Pat Shanley tells me I might get a job with the county council like he did. He says Friday is hiring day in Mullingar and gives me the address of their office at the Green Bridge.

Mammy says, "You're too young. You have to be either eighteen or twenty-one to get a job on the council."

Now Joe left behind a black leather topcoat in his haste to leave Moyvore. It's been hanging on the back of the door for ages, and I decide to try in on for size. The coat is a bit too wide at the shoulders, about six inches too long, and goes around me once and a half at the waist. Other than those inconveniences, it fits me grand, and I pull the belt tight to take care of the middle.

So every Friday I ride to Mullingar asking for a job, and the answer is always the same. "We aren't hiring this week." That in spite of the fact that I look like a grown man. This is due mostly to the fact that I rub some dirt on my face to make me look older, plus my well-fitted leather coat. But all is not lost, because another door opens for me.

They're laying a telephone cable from Dublin to the west of Ireland, and have brought it out as far as Rathconrath, which is about five miles from Moyvore. I stop and ask one of the men for a job. I think he must be important by the way he shouts at the other men. He tells me the only one he needs is a tea boy, if I'm interested. I say, "Yes, sir," and thus begins what turns out to be my last job in Ireland.

Now making tea for over twenty men twice a day is no small deal—especially when I have to collect sticks for fire from ditches that have already been picked clean. Anyway, I get off to a good start and the men seem happy enough with the way I make the tea. I use two big black kettles, and in one of them I put in the tea sugar and milk. The other kettle I make with just the tea, because some of the men don't take milk, and others don't take sugar. I stick with this job until we get down near Ballymahon, where I decide to give up being tea boy because the money is too small for the effort, and I decide to work digging trenches like the other men.

Now this proves harder than it looks. This same tall, lanky ganger with the red face and loud mouth steps off nine paces for each man to dig, three feet deep, and about a foot and a half wide. Each step is supposed to be one yard, but most of the men think the way he stretches his legs it's closer to a yard and a half. This amount must be dug by each man, come high hell or low water. If we come across a rock that's too big to remove, we dig under it as far as possible, go over it, and start on the other side, and the rock is left for blasting. But come rain or shine, it better be done. The first day my hands are all blistered and bleeding from the pick and shovel, and the paraffin oil doesn't do much good when I rub it on them.

The next day I wear two old socks with holes for the thumbs, and I survive another eight hours. I stick it out for a little over a week and then I can't take any more of this ignorant bastard standing on the bank shouting at me, so I tell him to go fuck himself and he fires me. When he hands me my pay at two o'clock, he tells me but for his position he'd give me a good beating. And looking at the size of him, and looking at me, I don't doubt that he could. A few weeks later I heard that a worker drove a pick through his foot accidentally on purpose.

Christmas comes and we have lots of everything, including a turkey. Next day there are but a few wren boys, mostly kids blowing on a mouth organ, and dancing to jigs poorly learned. Moyvore has gone so quiet it seems as though it's nearly deserted. No more pitch and toss, no more skittles or top flogging, And no more young colleens dancing at the crossroads to fulfill the dreams of Eamon De Valera. No, all that is gone, gone to fulfill the dark cloud of immigration.

Aunt Nellie comes to visit us, along with her son, Tommy Connell, by her first marriage. He decides he'll stay with us for a week before going back to England. Mammy thinks it's because he doesn't get along with his half brothers and sisters. They all have the same name because when his father Pat Connell died, his mother married Pat's brother, Ned.

Tommy is the life of the place, a good singer, and brings a lot of trade to MacAuley's pub. A lot of the girls are keen on him, and as he says himself he just plays them along, because he's already engaged to a nurse in England. I ask Tommy if he's sure he wouldn't mind taking me back to England with him, and he says, "No, not at all. Sure, aren't we cousins?" I wonder, will he be of the same mind in the morning?

There's plenty of drink in the house, and lots of neighbors willing to partake of it. Patsy Rodgers dances to jigs played on the fiddle by the fiddler Kincaid, of the Athlone Céili band. Seán Rodgers, not to outdone, plays tunes on the mouth organ and dances. Pat Shanley, as usual, insists on Mammy giving a recitation. She recites one about a blacksmith I haven't heard before. My brother Frank tells me it will be his turn to go to England in two years. Eddie pipes in, "If and when that time comes, don't expect me to entertain you before you go."

It's my last night at home and I barely get a wink of sleep with the party going till all hours, and Tommy singing every rebel song known to man, and begged for more. Morning comes, the goodbyes are said, and I walk out the gate, as ten others did before me. And the trend continues.

A Journey Begins

The train ride from Mullingar to Dublin's Houston station was uneventful, and likewise the short train ride from there to Dun Laoghaire and the boat. After all, what can one say about the crackle and clatter of a green painted train as it rolled along those rusty tracks on that wet and windy January of 1955? Or about the smoke and steam flying by the windows, or the lonesome whistle as the train chugged through small stations and railroad crossings?

I was three months short of my seventeenth birthday that wintry afternoon as I set out to follow in the footsteps of my older brothers and sisters. There was very little talking among the passengers, and still less by my cousin sitting next to me; he sat with his head in his hands as though in a dream, and like death warmed over.

I ask him, "Are you all right, Tommy?"

He turns his head up toward me with his bloodshot eyes and says, "For God's sake, leave me alone, man. I'm as sick as a small hospital." Then I wonder if that's how Daddy felt all those years after his drinking.

We get to the boat and stand in line near all the other passengers with suitcases and bags of every description, some with tears still wet on their faces, all waiting to board. It all gives me time to think of my mother and her somber goodbye, and wonder if there was a tear behind the brave front. Time to think of my younger brothers, Frank and Eddie, and their offered handshake with no show of emotion; and to realize that I offered that same handshake many a time to the others before me.

I think of my older brother, Tom, and how he never even came down to say goodbye, and I wonder if all the kids he fathers faithfully each year will have to leave as we did.

I thought of my father's last words to Dolly before she left. "If the time ever comes when you've no money and nowhere to stay, you can always come home. But if you ever get in the family way, don't ever show your face here."

And her answer to him. "Don't you worry, Daddy. I'm not that bad, or that stupid."

I thought about my own feelings and the anxiety, not only for what lay ahead, but also for what I would leave behind—of feelings buried so deep I couldn't express them in words; feelings of loss, loneliness, shame, and emptiness. Feelings of need and wanting to belong. All those I would carry with me on board, and they would remain with me for many a year, before I could recognize and learn how to deal with them.

As I walked up that gangplank of the princess Maud, a converted cattle ship, to take my first step on board, I knew it would be the first step of my adult journey. This new journey would take me to me many places. A journey of searching and seeking—not for what I'd lost, but for what I never had. A journey that began many years ago when Bridget McCann, shop girl, met Joseph Burke, blacksmith and farrier, an independent man of means, who swore he would never work for any man but himself, and so my Mammy said.

Printed in the United Kingdom
by Lightning Source UK Ltd.
107529UKS00002BB/2